CHARLES DICKENS

Charles Dickens was born in Portsmouth in 1812. He studied at Wellington House Academy and worked as a law clerk, court stenographer and shorthand reporter, which led to his first collection of pieces, *Sketches by Boz* (1836).

His major works include *The Pickwick Papers* (1836), *Oliver Twist* (1837–9), *Nicholas Nickleby* (1838–9), *A Christmas Carol* (1843), *Martin Chuzzlewit* (1843–4), *David Copperfield* (1849–50), *Bleak House* (1852–3), *Hard Times* (1854), *Little Dorrit* (1855–7), *A Tale of Two Cities* (1859), *Great Expectations* (1860–1), *Our Mutual Friend* (1864–5) and the unfinished *The Mystery of Edwin Drood* (1870), as well as other novels, books and short stories. None of his major works has ever gone out of print.

Dickens married Catherine Hogarth in 1836 and had ten children with her. He died in June 1870 from a stroke and, contrary to his wish to be buried in Rochester Cathedral, was buried in Poet's Corner of Westminster Abbey.

T0353194

MARK GATISS

Mark Gatiss has had a long and varied career as a writer and producer behind the camera, as well as being a critically acclaimed actor and published author. His early success on television was as part of the comedy troupe The League of Gentlemen, for which he both wrote and appeared on screen as various characters.

Mark is the co-creator and executive producer of *Sherlock*, the hit BBC series starring Benedict Cumberbatch and Martin Freeman, which has seen unprecedented global success, winning a total of nine Emmys and twelve BAFTAs across its four series.

Recent acting roles on screen include *The Father* alongside Anthony Hopkins and Olivia Colman, based on Florian Zeller's play of the same name, as the Duke of Marlborough in the BAFTA and Oscar-winning *The Favourite*, as Giles Winslow in Disney's *Christopher Robin*, as Robert Cecil in BBC One's *Gunpowder*, as Stephen Gardiner in *Wolf Hall* for the BBC, as Peter Mandelson in James Graham's *Coalition* for Channel Four, and as Tycho Nestoris in HBO's *Game of Thrones*.

On stage, he has starred alongside Tom Hiddleston in *Coriolanus*, as Harold in Mart Crowley's *The Boys in the Band*, as Doctor Shpigelsky in Patrick Marber's adaptation of Turgenev's *Three Days in the Country* for which he received the Olivier Award for Best Actor in a Supporting Role, and the title role in Alan Bennett's *The Madness of George III* at Nottingham Playhouse.

He was the co-creator and executive producer of the BBC and Netflix drama *Dracula*. He has also written and directed adaptations of several M. R. James' stories for the BBC, and *The Amazing Mr Blunden* starring Simon Callow and Tamsin Greig (Sky, Christmas 2021).

Charles Dickens

A CHRISTMAS CAROL –
A GHOST STORY

adapted for the stage by
Mark Gatiss

NICK HERN BOOKS
London
www.nickhernbooks.co.uk

A Nick Hern Book   ·

This adaptation of *A Christmas Carol – A Ghost Story* first published in
Great Britain as a paperback original in 2021 by Nick Hern Books Limited,
The Glasshouse, 49a Goldhawk Road, London W12 8QP

A Christmas Carol – A Ghost Story copyright © 2021 Mark Gatiss

Mark Gatiss has asserted his right to be identified as the author of this
adaptation

Cover image: **feast**creative.com

Designed and typeset by Nick Hern Books, London
Printed in Great Britain by Mimeo Ltd, Huntingdon, Cambridgeshire PE29 6XX

A CIP catalogue record for this book is available from the British Library

ISBN 978 1 83904 056 6

Woodland
CARBON
www.woodlandcarbon.co.uk
NICK HERN BOOKS
Printed on Carbon Captured paper

Introduction
Mark Gatiss

'Christmas,' wrote Charles Dickens' daughter 'was always a time which in our home was looked forward to with eagerness and delight. And to my father it was a time dearer than any other part of the year.'

The sheer power and joy of Dickens' story – and the restless energy with which it was produced – has ensured that the tale of Ebenezer Scrooge and his ghostly visitors has assumed the quality of myth. It's also, from its inception, proven incredibly popular to dramatise. So why another version?

I've been obsessed with *A Christmas Carol* since I was four years old and went to see the Albert Finney film at my local Odeon. Well, my first actual encounter with the story had actually been *Carry On Christmas* on TV the year before! But I can vividly remember sitting in the red plush (ish) seats of the cinema knowing that *this* was going to be the real thing. The proper scary story. And being, frankly, terrified in anticipation. The film left a profound impression on me, made even stronger by seeing, in short order, the brilliant Alistair Sim version and Richard Williams' beautiful short cartoon.

Something about the story spoke deeply to me, as it has to generation after generation. Its combination of optimism, sentiment, pain and melancholy, all somehow, magically, combined into the perfect Christmas story. Bitter-sweet, indeed, like Christmas itself. When I finally read Dickens' actual story I was knocked out. Not just by the genuine jollity and warmth (it is a *carol* after all, divided not into chapters but into staves), but by its sheer power. Righteous anger courses throughout and certain passages – Bob Cratchit breaking down sitting at the bedside of his dead son, the terrifying Children, Ignorance and Want – remain long in the memory. But there's something else, something which lies at the heart of my adaptation. Because while it's true to say that this wonderful story in many ways reinvented the traditions of Christmas and the popular appetite for them, it's also true that its status as a *ghost story* has been somewhat undervalued.

There had been ghosts before *A Christmas Carol*, of course, but being the literary magician that he was, Dickens somehow contrived to concentrate an entire, very English tradition into one story. The doomed and repentant Jacob Marley is the closest we have to a revenant, a spectral visitor returned from the grave, clanking his chains and owing, I would say, a substantial debt to the ghost of Hamlet's father.

Christmas Past, is described as a 'strange figure… like a child but not so like a child as like an old man', constantly receding and approaching from sight with a blazing light burning from its head. It seems to represent memory itself, blurring and shifting unreliably, stirring up old wounds and old joys.

Christmas Present is an altogether different proposition, seeming to tap into a more Pagan Christmas: a great substantial, rather terrifying lover of life. A ghost of appetites, sprinkling kindness from its burning torch yet, within its massive frame, also sheltering Mankind's neglected children, which cling to it for refuge.

And Christmas Yet to Come, whom Scrooge fears more than all the others, is a dark spectral shape, as unknowable as the future. Often characterised as Death itself, the Ghost actually possesses a very human hand, not a skeletal claw, which ultimately trembles as though moved by Scrooge's final entreaties.

These four spectres form the spine of the narrative, taking Scrooge on his epic journey from 'covetous old sinner' to the redeemed soul we see at the end. But the story teems with ghosts. The ghosts of regret and lost love, of broken friendships and ignorant mistakes, of heartbreak and loss. In this adaptation, amongst the 'pleasing terrors' of an evening spent in spectral company, I hope we will all find our own joys and restored hopes, seeing in Ebenezer Scrooge that it's *never* too late.

There is an old proverb. The best time to plant a tree was twenty years ago. The second best time… is now.

Merry Christmas!

This adaptation of *A Christmas Carol – A Ghost Story* by Mark Gatiss was commissioned by Nottingham Playhouse and first performed there on 2 November 2021 (previews from 29 October), with the following cast and creative team:

EBENEZER SCROOGE	Nicholas Farrell
JACOB MARLEY	Mark Gatiss
FRED	James Backway
CAROLINE	Angelina Chudi
GHOST OF CHRISTMAS PAST	Jo Eaton-Kent
TINY TIM	Zak Ford-Williams
BELLE	Aoife Gaston
NARRATOR	Christopher Godwin
BOB CRATCHIT	Edward Harrison
MRS CRATCHIT	Sarah Ridgeway
GHOST OF CHRISTMAS PRESENT	Joe Shire
GRACE CRATCHIT	Renae Rhodes/ Esmé Tchoudi
EDWIN CRATCHIT	Lauren Tanner/ Charlie Westlake

Director	Adam Penford
Designer	Paul Wills
Lighting Designer	Philip Gladwell
Sound Designer	Ella Wahlström
Video Designer	Nina Dunn
Movement Director	Georgina Lamb
Composer	Tingying Dong
Illusion Designer	John Bulleid
Illusion Designer Associate	Will Houstoun
Casting Director	Sam Stevenson CDG
Puppet Designer & Director	Matthew Forbes
Musical Director	Tom Attwood
Voice Coach	Kay Welch
Associate Director	Jasmine Teo

Costume Supervisor	Joan Hughes
Wig and Make Up Supervisor	Moira O'Connell
Head Production Video Engineer	Harrison Cooke
& Video Programmer	
Production Managers	Andy Bartlett, Pete Kramer
Company & Stage Manager	Jane Eliot-Webb
Deputy Stage Manager	Ruthie Philip-Smith
Assistant Stage Managers	Olly Holmes,
	Louise Pearson

The production transferred to Alexandra Palace Theatre,
London, from 26 November 2021, produced by Eleanor Lloyd
Productions and Eilene Davidson Productions, with the
following changes to the cast and creative team:

GRACE CRATCHIT	Eilah Jaffar/
	Evie Miller/
	Jasmine Nyenya
EDWIN CRATCHIT	Kaylenn Aires Fonseca/
	Sonny Fowler/
	Xavier Wilkins

Company Stage Manager	Michela Brennan
Deputy Stage Manager	Ruthie Philip-Smith
Assistant Stage Managers	Tash Holdaway,
	Mark Smith
Sound No. 1	Martin Curtis
Sound No. 2	Emily Coley
Wardrobe Manager	Lisa Brindley
Wardrobe Deputy	Paige Davey

Supported using public funding by
ARTS COUNCIL
LOTTERY FUNDED **ENGLAND**

Characters

JACOB MARLEY
BOB CRATCHIT
EBENEZER SCROOGE
NARRATOR
FRED
MISS DIMPLE
MRS BOONE
A BLIND MAN
TOM
BONNIFACE
GHOST OF CHRISTMAS
   PAST
YOUNG SCROOGE
FAN
MR THRUMPHULL
POSTBOY
FEZZIWIG
YOUNG MARLEY
MRS FEZZIWIG
MR BOUNCER
BELLE
FATHER
CHILD
GHOST OF CHRISTMAS
   PRESENT
WAITER
SECOND WAITER
MRS CRATCHIT
BELINDA CRATCHIT
PETER CRATCHIT
EDWIN CRATCHIT
GRACE CRATCHIT
MARTHA CRATCHIT

TINY TIM
KEEPER 1
KEEPER 2
HELMSMAN
SEAMAN
CAROLINE
TOPPER
POLL
MISS CHOKEPEAR
MR CHOKEPEAR
MR GRUB
MISS GRUB
IGNORANCE
WANT
GHOST OF CHRISTMAS
   YET TO COME
PLUMCHUTE
GIPP
TOTTERALL
OLD JOE
MRS DILBER
MR THURSDAY
MRS CHITTY
MR BOSWICK
MRS BOSWICK
BOY
PARLOUR MAID
ELDERLY WOMAN

11

And a SKINNY BOY, BOYS THROWING SNOWBALLS,
A WRETCHED WOMAN *and baby,* PHANTOMS, *a* GHOST
IN A WHITE WAISTCOAT, SCHOOLBOYS, *a* FIDDLER,
MRS FEZZIWIG*'s* DAUGHTERS, WORKMEN, BELLE*'s*
CHILDREN, *a* MINER, PARTY GUESTS, BOSWICK
CHILDREN

This text went to press before the end of rehearsals and so may differ slightly from the play as performed.

ACT ONE

Scene One

Darkness. Darkness that gradually opens out to reveal a low, gloomy, coffin-black counting house, its corners softened into shadow. Every shelf crammed with mouldering papers, files and ledgers – like bad teeth in a rotten mouth.

And there, perched on a high stool at a high desk, is a withered man. His spectacles are on his forehead and he's burning a stick of wax over a candle-flame.

The candle's almost spent.

He seals the wax with his signet ring and looks up.

MARLEY. Cratchit!

> *There's a a scrambling from the outer office and* BOB CRATCHIT *tumbles in. He's scrawny and fairly blue with cold.*

BOB. Yes, sir?

MARLEY. Correspondence. The matter of Unwin, Chatterham and Penge. You'll just make the last post.

> *He tosses the sealed letter and a pile of others at his clerk.*

BOB. Begging your pardon, sir. But, you're forgetting…

MARLEY. I am?

BOB. Last post's gone, sir. Early. On account of the season.

MARLEY. *Season?*

BOB. Christmas, sir!

> MARLEY *narrows his eyes, opens his mouth to respond when, from somewhere in the office, as though a phantom has spoken, comes the cry:*

SCROOGE. *Humbug!!*

The withered man – JACOB MARLEY *– smiles, a horrible, basilisk smile.*

MARLEY. As my esteemed partner would have it, Cratchit. Humbug!

BOB. Yes, Mr Marley. Humbug, sir. I'm sure, sir. Yes, sir.

Lights up on the adjacent office which abuts MARLEY'*s. It's almost a duplicate. At his high desk, his face buried in ledgers is* EBENEZER SCROOGE.

SCROOGE. You'll deliver those letters by hand, Cratchit.

BOB. All of them, Mr Scrooge?

SCROOGE. Every. Single. One.

BOB. But it's almost seven, sir. And Christmas Eve…

SCROOGE *looks up, quill poised. He's crabbed, gimlet-eyed, a mouth like a dog's arse.*

SCROOGE (*contemptuously*). *Christmas Eve.* And you'll want the whole day off tomorrow?

BOB. If… quite convenient, sir.

SCROOGE. It's not convenient. And it's not fair. If we were to stop you half a crown for it, you'd think yourself ill-used, I'll be bound!

BOB. It is only once a year, sir.

SCROOGE. A poor excuse for picking a man's pocket every twenty-fifth of December. Eh, Jacob?

MARLEY. Well put, Ebeneezer. *Christmas!* Hum–

SCROOGE. –bug!

SCROOGE *fixes* BOB *with an unwavering stare.*

You'll despatch every last one of those letters, Cratchit. And only then may you get yourself home for your… *celebrations.*

BOB. Yes, sir.

In a flurry, BOB *scrambles into his long scarf and claps his battered hat onto his head.*

Goodnight, Mr Scrooge. Mr Marley. A merry –

SCROOGE *and* MARLEY *look up simultaneously. The words die on* BOB*'s lips and he hurries out.*

There's a blast of freezing air and snowflakes from the door.

MARLEY. A merry Christmas!

SCROOGE. And him a clerk on fifteen shillings a week! We have only ourselves to blame, Jacob. Out of misguided altruism we employ wretches such as Cratchit – yet do they attempt to rise above their miserable station? Do they grasp their opportunities as we did? Nay! What that lazy fellow needs is his wits sharpening. What do you say? A reduction in salary? *Thirteen* shillings a week?

MARLEY. Twelve?

SCROOGE. Eleven?

MARLEY. *Ten?*

SCROOGE. Ten! A nice round figure, eh, Jacob?

They both chuckle mirthlessly. Then MARLEY *gives a little gasp of pain. He clutches his arm, then his chest. His quill flutters to the floor. In the other office,* SCROOGE *is oblivious.*

Do you want to break the happy news, Jacob, or shall I?

Jacob?

No response.

Jacob?

No response.

He gets up and shuffles into MARLEY*'s office.*

MARLEY *lies stretched across his desk.*

Dead as a coffin nail.

SCROOGE *feels for a pulse. Gives a grunt. Not a flicker of emotion passes over his face.*

He snuffs out the little candle by the side of the desk.

SCROOGE. Waste not, want not.

Scene Two

A wintry wind howls over the scene. And over the sign hanging outside the offices. 'SCROOGE and MARLEY', gold on ebony. It's enveloped in freezing fog and begins to age. The wood cracks, the letters fade.

NARRATOR (*voice-over*). Marley was dead. To begin with. This must be distinctly understood or nothing wonderful can come of the story I am going to tell you.

Lights up on an elderly man – our NARRATOR. *He's sitting in a leather armchair, wearing an Edwardian smoking jacket and slippers.*

Old Marley was as dead as a door nail. Or a coffin nail, if you want to be particular. Scrooge never painted out Marley's name. There it stood, years afterwards, above their place of business. Sometimes people new to the firm called Scrooge Scrooge – and sometimes Marley. But he answered to both names. It was all the same to him.

We now see something of the cramped court in which the office stands. A poulterer's shop, a pawn-broker's, solicitor's offices, etc.

We're vaguely aware of people hurrying back and forth, a blur of bonnets and stovepipe hats.

Freezing fog. Cold, bleak, biting. Somewhere a church clock strikes three.

A SKINNY BOY *is standing outside on the office steps singing 'God Rest Ye Merry, Gentlemen'.*

BOB, *visible through a frosty window, gives him a warm smile and, encouraged, the* SKINNY BOY *bends down at the keyhole and sings louder.*

The door is suddenly thrown open and SCROOGE *is revealed. He's older, greyer, even more pinched and holding a huge steel ruler in his hand.*

THWACK! He cracks the SKINNY BOY *across the back with it and the child scurries off, whimpering in pain.*

NARRATOR. Oh! But he was a tight-fisted hand at the grindstone was Ebenezer Scrooge! A squeezing, wrenching, grasping, scraping, clutching, covetous, old sinner! Hard and sharp as flint, from which no steel had ever struck out generous fire. Secret, self-contained and solitary as an oyster! He carried his own low temperature always about with him, he iced his office in the dog-days of summer and didn't thaw it one degree at Christmas.

SCROOGE *slams the door just as* FRED – *a handsome man in his thirties – emerges from the shroud of fog.*

He reacts to the slammed door, then takes a deep breath.

Scene Three

SCROOGE *stalks back to his office. The door of* MARLEY*'s office is closed, though his name has not been painted over on the frosted glass.*

SCROOGE *glares at* BOB *who is trying to warm himself at his feeble fire.*

SCROOGE. Resting merrily enough, Cratchit?

BOB. N… no, sir! Sorry, Mr Scrooge!

He grabs his long white scarf from the hat-stand and wraps it round and round his neck. The front door flies open and FRED *bounds in, all good humour.*

FRED. A merry Christmas, Uncle!

SCROOGE *darts into his office and slams the door in* FRED*'s face.*

...God save you!

FRED *and* BOB *exchange a look. Then* FRED *throws open the door, undaunted.*

SCROOGE. God save me indeed, from such as you, nephew. A *merry* Christmas! Bah! Humbug!

FRED. You don't mean that, I'm sure.

SCROOGE. I do. What right have you to be merry? You're poor enough.

FRED (*laughing*). What right have you to be dismal? You're rich enough!

SCROOGE. That I am! And through my own graft! Out upon a merry Christmas, you young fool. What's Christmas but a time for paying bills without money; a time for finding yourself a year older, but not an hour richer?

FRED. Don't be cross, Uncle...

SCROOGE. If I could work my will, every idiot who goes about with 'Merry Christmas' on his lips should be boiled with his own pudding.

FRED. Uncle!

SCROOGE. And buried in the centre of four lonely roads with a stake of holly through his heart!

FRED. *Uncle!*

SCROOGE. He should! Keep Christmas in your own way and let me keep it in mine.

FRED. But you don't keep it!

SCROOGE (*low, dangerous*). Then let me leave it alone.

FRED. There are many things from which I have derived good without *profiting*. But I've always thought of Christmas as a good time. A kind, forgiving, charitable time. The only time in the long calendar of the year, when men and women seem by one consent to open their shut-up hearts freely, and to think of people below them as if they really were fellow-travellers to the grave.

In the outer office, BOB *listens attentively.*

And therefore, Uncle, though it has never put a scrap of gold in my pocket, I believe that it has done me good, and will do me good and I say, God bless it!

BOB *starts applauding, then stops as* SCROOGE *glares through the open door at him.*

SCROOGE. Another sound from you, Cratchit, and you'll keep your Christmas by losing your situation!

BOB (*to* FRED). You're quite a powerful speaker, sir. I wonder you don't go into parliament.

FRED. I might at that!

SCROOGE. Just what that place needs. Another popinjay!

FRED. Come, dine with us tomorrow.

SCROOGE. Us?

FRED. With my wife and me.

SCROOGE. Your *wife*. Saddled with such baggage at your age and, no doubt, a gaggle of hungry mouths on the way. You'll have children – boys. Those boys will grow up bad, of course. And run wild in the street without shoes or stockings!

FRED. Good heavens, I trust not!

SCROOGE. Why on Earth did you marry?

FRED. Because I fell in love!

SCROOGE *shakes his head.*

SCROOGE. I'll retire to Bedlam. Good afternoon!

FRED. I want nothing from you, Uncle. I ask nothing of you.
Why can't we be friends? Mother would've wanted –

SCROOGE *winces. A moment between them.*

SCROOGE *(quiet)*. Good afternoon.

FRED. I am sorry, with all my heart, to find you so resolute.
But I've made the trial in homage to Christmas, and I'll
keep my Christmas humour to the last. So a Merry
Christmas, Uncle!

SCROOGE. Good afternoon!

FRED *(sings)*. And a Happy New Year!

SCROOGE. *Good afternoon!*

Back in the outer office, FRED *pulls a face for the benefit of*
BOB, *who smiles back.*

FRED. Well, Mr Cratchit. I know I can rely on a warmer
welcome this side of my uncle's door, eh?

BOB. Indeed, sir!

FRED. And what of your plans for the great day?

BOB. The usual, sir. All the family round to Camden Town. My
Martha's quite the young lady now and is 'prenticed at a
milliner's. And I've an eye on a situation for young Peter
that would be of great help to the whole family. Things…
being a wee bit tight.

FRED *(thoughtfully)*. Yes, indeed.

And the little fellow? Tim?

BOB. Oh. He is well, sir. Quite well.

BOB *glances down.*

FRED. Mightily glad to hear it.

Two ladies appear at the front door, MISS DIMPLE *and*
MRS BOONE.

MISS DIMPLE *is rather fluttery and nervous,* MRS BOONE *considerably more forthright – an inveterate organiser of jumble sales.*

MRS BOONE. Scrooge and Marley's?

FRED *points to* SCROOGE*'s office.*

FRED. Through there. And the best of luck!

(*Sotto.*) Merry Christmas, Mr Cratchit!

BOB (*sotto*). *Merry Christmas, sir!*

FRED *sweeps out.*

MISS BOONE *marches into* SCROOGE*'s office.*

MRS BOONE. Mr Scrooge, is it? Or Mr Marley?

SCROOGE *doesn't look up from his ledger.*

SCROOGE. Mr Marley has been dead these seven years…

MISS DIMPLE. Oh dear.

SCROOGE. He died…

The thought suddenly strikes him.

…seven years ago this very night.

MRS BOONE (*beaming*). Awfully sorry, I'm sure. But no doubt his generosity is well represented by his surviving partner?

SCROOGE (*steely*). As to that, ladies, you may rest assured.

The ladies beam, pleased.

MRS BOONE. You see, at this time of the year, Mr Scrooge, this festive season, we like to do what we can to provide for the poor and destitute. As you can imagine, they suffer greatly.

MISS DIMPLE. Fings being what they are.

MRS BOONE (*sadly*). Yes.

MISS DIMPLE. Many thousands are in want of common necessaries. Food. Shelter. Hundreds of thousands are in want of common comforts –

MRS BOONE. And – oh! – how little is required to throw a modicum of sunshine. To be kind.

SCROOGE*'s pen scratches on.*

SCROOGE. Are there no prisons?

MISS DIMPLE. Plenty of prisons.

SCROOGE. And the Union workhouses? Are they still in operation?

MRS BOONE. They are, sir. Still. I wish I could say they were not.

SCROOGE. The Treadmill and the Poor Law. In full vigour?

MISS DIMPLE (*sighing*). Both very busy, sir.

SCROOGE. I'm very glad to hear it! I was afraid for a moment that something had occurred to stop them in their useful course.

The ladies exchanged puzzled looks.

MISS DIMPLE. I think you misunderstand us, Mr Scrooge. We're trying to raise money. To buy the poor some food, and means of warmth.

MRS BOONE. We choose this time, because it is a time, of all others, when want is keenly felt, and abundance rejoices. What shall we put you down for?

SCROOGE. Nothing!

MISS DIMPLE (*nodding sagely*). You wish to be anonymous?

SCROOGE. *I wish to be left alone!* Since you ask me what I wish, that is my answer.

I don't make merry myself at Christmas and I can't afford to make idle people merry. I help to support the establishments I have mentioned. They cost enough – and those who are badly off must go there.

MISS DIMPLE. Many can't go there.

MRS BOONE. And many would rather die.

SCROOGE (*hissing*). If they would rather die, they had better do it, and decrease the surplus population.

MISS DIMPLE (*shocked*). *Sir!*

SCROOGE. The poor have no earthly right or business to be born! *My* business occupies me constantly. Good afternoon.

MISS DIMPLE and MRS BOONE go out, shaking their heads.

Scene Four

NARRATOR. And so the bleak, dark day passed into night. The ancient tower of a church, whose gruff old bell was always peeping slyly down at Scrooge out of a Gothic window in the wall, became invisible, and struck the hours and quarters in the clouds, with tremulous vibrations afterwards as if its teeth were chattering in its frozen head up there. The cold became intense.

A BLIND MAN stumbles through the fog with his dog.

BLIND MAN. Alms for the blind! Alms for the blind!

A brazier sputters in the square close by and a knot of MEN and BOYS are gathered around it, trying desperately to get warm.

TOM. Evening, John!

A poulterer, TOM, comes out of his shop and presses a tankard of hot posset into the BLIND MAN's hands.

BLIND MAN. Hello, Tom!

TOM tickles the dog under its chin. It happily wags its tail. Then TOM guides the BLIND MAN to the brazier.

TOM. Let's get you warm, now.

Some of the BOYS are throwing snowballs across the court, laughing hysterically.

Scene Five

In the office, BOB *looks up expectantly as the church clock chimes.* SCROOGE *waits until the last stroke of seven, then gives a barely perceptible nod.*

BOB *has his hat on in a moment and snuffs out his candle.*

SCROOGE *clambers laboriously into his own, moth-eaten coat.*

SCROOGE. You'll want all day tomorrow, I suppose?

BOB *sighs. They go through this every year.*

BOB (*flatly*). If quite convenient, sir.

SCROOGE. It is never convenient! A day's wages for no work! But I suppose you must have the whole day. Be here all the earlier next morning –

He breaks off suddenly. In MARLEY*'s long disused office he seems to see the silhouette of a man.*

It moves.

SCROOGE *stares, then darts forward, throwing open the door.*

The office beyond is dark and crowded with ledgers.

A quill pen in the inkwell seems to move of its own accord – then stops.

SCROOGE *makes to go – then a ledger falls to the floor, making him jump.*

BOB *is looking at* SCROOGE *with a weak smile.*
SCROOGE *claps his hat on and stalks out of the office and into the fog. He exits. Outside…*

BLIND MAN. Alms for the blind!

The BLIND MAN *is aware of someone there.*

Alms for the blind, my friend?

SCROOGE shoots him a withering look. Then he notices a few coins in the collecting box around the BLIND MAN*'s neck.*

He looks about shiftily then carefully reaches down to pluck them out.

The BLIND MAN*'s dog growls.* SCROOGE *lingers a moment and then backs off with a scowl, disappearing into the fog…*

BOB *locks the office door and finds a pewter tankard thrust straight into his hand as he turns.*

TOM. Here you go, my buck. And compliments of the season!

BOB. Ha, ha! Thank'ee, Tom. And to you!

He gazes past his friend at the BOYS *throwing snowballs.*

You any good?

TOM. About as good as a patent mackintosh in a deluge but willin' to try!

BOB. Ha, ha! Come on then.

He hands the tankard back to TOM *and starts making a snowball. One of the* BOYS *pelts him. He laughs – and then returns fire.*

Hello! Below there!

Scene Six

SCROOGE *gropes his way down a fog-shrouded street.*

Suddenly, a figure looms out of the darkness. A worried-looking cab-driver, BONNIFACE.

BONNIFACE. Mr Scrooge! If I may have a word –

SCROOGE. Eh? Who are you?

BONNIFACE. Edward Bonniface, sir. You'll recall –

SCROOGE. I do. Indeed I do. A little matter of seven pounds, three shillings and six.

BONNIFACE. My youngest was taken wery bad, sir, with the scarlet fever, and we had nothing put by to pay for the doctors –

SCROOGE. Spare me your tedious narrative, sir. Repayment of the loan falls due in two days, does it not?

BONNIFACE *nods slowly.*

BONNIFACE. I must have more time, sir.

SCROOGE (*he hears it every day*). *More time?*

BONNIFACE. Yes, sir. I'm working on the Hackney-coaches till I don't know what o'clock just to make ends meet and the missus is doing her bit too. Another fortnight and we'll be able to –

SCROOGE. Two days, Mr Bonniface. Seven pounds, three shillings and six. I can make no exceptions.

A tremor of terror runs through BONNIFACE.

BONNIFACE. I cannot do it, sir! And if I cannot pay I… I shall go to prison!

SCROOGE. Then, pray, do not let me detain you. You will be able to provide your own transportation at least. Haha.

BONNIFACE *falls to his knees and clutches at* SCROOGE's *leg.*

BONNIFACE. For Christ's sake, Mr Scrooge. Show mercy!

SCROOGE. Get up!

BONNIFACE. It is Christmas! For the sake of him whose name we honour, show a little charity.

SCROOGE. Get up! Get up, you ridiculous little man. Or would you prefer I raise the debt higher?

BONNIFACE *gives a wild look then scrambles to his feet and flees.*

NARRATOR. Scrooge lived in chambers which had once belonged to his deceased partner, Marley. They were a gloomy suite of rooms, in a lowering pile of buildings up a yard, where it had so little business to be, that one could scarcely help fancying it must have run there when it was a young house, playing at hide-and-seek with other houses, and forgotten the way out again. The yard was so dark that even Scrooge, who knew its every stone, was fain to grope with his hands...

TING!

Something rolls across the floor towards SCROOGE. *He starts. It's a big, heavy penny piece. It spins and spins and then falls. A little baffled,* SCROOGE *picks it up and pockets it.*

At last he finds his way to his front door. It's old and black and splintered like a coffin lid with a tarnished lion's head knocker.

SCROOGE *stoops to the huge ring of rusting keys at his waist and lifts one to the lock. He concentrates on shoving the key in and when he looks down, the knocker has changed!*

It's glowing with a strange, dismal light – like a bad lobster in a dark cellar – and it's not a lion's head but the face of JACOB MARLEY!

His spectacles are on his forehead and his hair stirring about as though wafted by hot air. But his eyes stare fixedly, dreadfully ahead. Or, rather, one eye does. In the other eye, a big penny, the brother of the one which rolled over the ground.

TING!

The coin pops from MARLEY's *eye. On the keening wind,* SCROOGE *seems to hear…*

MARLEY. Scroooooooooge…

SCROOGE *claps his hand to his mouth – blinks – and the knocker is suddenly only a knocker once more.*

SCROOGE *scrabbles at the lock and lets himself inside.*

SCROOGE. *Humbug!*

Scene Seven

Slamming the door behind him, SCROOGE *reaches for a candle-stick.*

The echo of the door reverberates through the darkness.

Slightly panicked, SCROOGE *struggles to light a match.*

When the flaring flame is finally alight he examines the back of the door as though expecting to see the back of MARLEY's *head.*

Nothing there.

SCROOGE *shakes his head and runs his hand over his fevered brow.*

He scurries towards the dangerous-looking stair, his shadow leaping hugely over the weeping plaster of the wall.

SCROOGE *stops on the bottom stair and freezes.*

There's a strange noise from somewhere close. It's like the tinkling of falling icicles or the jangling of horse-brasses.

SCROOGE *turns and a ghostly hearse is suddenly thundering towards him! It's driver-less but pulled along by skeletal horses, wisps of grave-begrimed material hanging from their bones.*

They plunge and whinny nightmarishly, their empty, huge-socketed eyes seeming to bore into SCROOGE's *own.*

SCROOGE *buries his face in his hands and the hearse goes right through him, mounting the stairs and vanishing into the ether.*

With no more ado, SCROOGE *races upstairs into his rooms…*

Scene Eight

SCROOGE *slams and double-locks the door behind him.*

He catches his breath, then shoots two bolts into place, badly frightened.

SCROOGE. Some disorder of the stomach, I warrant! A bit of bad beef… A blot of mustard…

But he isn't convincing himself. A gust of wind rattles the door and SCROOGE *retreats into the gloom, lights fading on him.*

Vignetted to one side of the stage – A WRETCHED WOMAN *and her baby are holed up against the bitter weather in a doorway opposite* SCROOGE's *lodgings. Snow is falling in huge flakes the size of chrysanthemums.*

We find SCROOGE *in his nightshirt, sitting with a candle by his meagre hearth where a pan of gruel is bubbling.*

And the fire sputters. A draft seems to come down the chimney and on it, the voice of MARLEY…

MARLEY. Scroooooooge… .

SCROOGE *starts and suddenly –*

– a bell rings.

He shoots a glance upwards to where several long disused servant's bells hang. They connect to some part of the house long-forgotten. But now one of them's ringing. Then another.

Then another. A dreadful, clamorous din.

SCROOGE *puts his hands over his ears and sinks into his chair, terrified.*

And the bells stop as suddenly as they began.

SCROOGE *tentatively removes his hands from his ears, then wishes he hadn't. For far below, in the deep cellars of the house, something stirs...*

Clank-clank-clank. Like chains being dragged.

SCROOGE *closes his eyes and wills it to go away.*

The muffled bang of the cellar door being flung open.

SCROOGE *whimpers.*

Then the awful sound of heavy footsteps on the stairs, dragging the chain behind them...

THUMP

THUMP

THUMP.

SCROOGE. It's humbug still! I won't... I won't believe it!

THUMP.

And then a terrible pause. There's something waiting on the other side of the door.

SCROOGE *can hear his own heart banging in his chest.*

SCROOGE *waits, appallingly afraid.*

Then he gasps in pure terror as MARLEY*'s ghost strides right through the locked door!*

The candle flame leaps up and goes out so the room is lit only by the fire and the ghastly green light of the phantom.

MARLEY *is dressed as we last saw him but a spectral white. Around his head is a tightly wrapped bandage and around his body is a massive steel chain made entirely of cash-boxes, deeds, ledgers and keys.*

The ghost looks straight at SCROOGE *yet its dead eyes do not flicker. It shifts and stirs about – creaking like an old ship – as though agitated by an unseen wind. It's a genuinely horrible sight.*

(*Feigned boldness.*) How now! What do you want with me?

MARLEY *pulls the winding bandage from his head and his jaw clacks open, falling right onto his breast in a Munch-like howl. His voice is grave-deep, hollow, awful.*

MARLEY. *MUCH!*

SCROOGE. Who are you?

MARLEY. Ask me who I was.

SCROOGE. Who *were* you then? Most pedantic for a ghost! (*Tries a laugh but it sounds feeble.*)

MARLEY. In life I was your partner, Jacob Marley.

SCROOGE. Jacob! Can… *can* you sit down?

MARLEY. I can.

SCROOGE. Do it, then.

MARLEY *does so, then inclines his head.*

MARLEY. You don't believe in me.

SCROOGE. I don't. I have read about such phantasms. Why, a slight disorder of the stomach can affect the senses. You see that toothpick?

MARLEY. I do.

SCROOGE. You're not looking at it.

MARLEY. But I see it notwithstanding.

SCROOGE. Well! I have but to swallow it, and be for the rest of my days persecuted by a legion of goblins, all of my own creation. You're no more than a fragment of underdone potato. There's… there's more of gravy than the grave about YOU!

He laughs but then throws himself to the floor as MARLEY *rises into the air terrifyingly, clanking and shaking his chains in fury.*

Oh Glory! Mercy!

MARLEY. Man of the worldly mind! Do you believe in me or not?

SCROOGE *puts his hands together as though praying.*

SCROOGE. I do! I must! But why... why have you come to me?

MARLEY. It is required of every man that the spirit within him should walk abroad among his fellow-men. If that spirit goes not forth in life, it is condemned to do so after death.

MARLEY *utters a dreadful cry and rattles his chains.*

It is doomed to wander through the world – oh, woe is me! – and witness what it cannot share, but *might* have shared on earth, and turned to happiness!

SCROOGE *points a shaking hand at* MARLEY*'s chains.*

SCROOGE. You... you are fettered. Why?

MARLEY. I wear the chain I forged in life. I made it link by link, and yard by yard. I girded it on of my own free will, and of my own free will I wore it. Is its pattern strange to you?

SCROOGE. What... what do you mean?

MARLEY. Or would you know the weight and length of the strong coil you bear yourself? It was full as heavy and as long as this seven Christmas Eves ago. You have laboured on it, since. It is a PONDEROUS chain!

SCROOGE *looks about him as though expecting to see the chain.*

SCROOGE. But, Jacob, you were always a good man of business...

MARLEY (*shrieking*). *BUSINESS!* Mankind was my business! Charity, mercy and benevolence were all my business. At this time of the rolling year, I suffer most. Why did I walk through crowds of fellow-beings with my eyes turned down, and never raise them to that blessed star which led the Wise Men to a poor abode?

Were there no poor homes to which its light would have conducted me!

He shudders and draws back towards the door.

I cannot rest, I cannot stay, I cannot linger... anywhere...

Hear me! My time is nearly gone.

SCROOGE. Tell me more. Speak comfort to me, Jacob!

MARLEY. I have none to give.

He makes to leave, then stops.

Save this. You have yet a chance and hope of escaping my fate. A chance and hope of my procuring, Ebenezer Scrooge.

SCROOGE. You were always a good friend to me.

MARLEY. You will be visited by three spirits.

SCROOGE. Is that the chance and hope you mentioned, Jacob?

MARLEY. It is.

SCROOGE. Then I... I think I'd rather not.

MARLEY. Without their visits, you cannot hope to shun the path I tread. Expect the first tomorrow, when the bell tolls one.

SCROOGE. Couldn't I take 'em all at once, and have it over with, Jacob?

MARLEY. Expect the second on the next night at the same hour. The third upon the next night when the last stroke of twelve has ceased to vibrate.

Remember what has passed between us, Ebenezer Scrooge. Look to see me... no more...

MARLEY *shoves his jaw back into place with a horrible click and wraps the winding bandage round his chin again, walking backwards into the shadows and pointing towards the window.*

Suddenly, SCROOGE *can hear nothing but a wretched moaning and sobbing.*

MARLEY *listens sorrowfully and then... is gone.*

SCROOGE *advances gingerly and looks out. The air is filled with* PHANTOMS, *hopeless, wretched, damned. All of them are chained like* MARLEY's *ghost.*

They are all desperately trying to help the destitute PEOPLE *who huddle in the freezing streets.*

A GHOST IN A WHITE WAISTCOAT, *with a massive safe chained to his ankle, is trying to help the* WRETCHED WOMAN *and her baby but to no avail.*

SCROOGE *screws his eyes shut and gradually the moaning fades.*

The tick of his clock becomes audible. He turns round and the candle is alight again. He glances out of the window but can see only the vague shapes of the poor through the frost-crazed pane.

He shuffles back into the room.

He enters his bedroom and looks about fearfully, shakes his head.

SCROOGE. Bah! Hum...

He looks under the bed.

(Softly.)...bug.

He gets into bed and draws the curtains around him.

ACT TWO

Scene One

NARRATOR. When Scrooge awoke, it was so dark, that looking out of bed, he could scarcely distinguish the transparent window from the opaque walls of his chamber. He was endeavouring to pierce the darkness with his ferret eyes, when the chimes of a neighbouring church struck the four quarters. So he listened for the hour.

SCROOGE. Six o'clock...

Seven?

SCROOGE*'s eyes snap open. He peers into the darkness.*

But the bell tolls on.

And again.

Eight o'clock? It isn't possible. It was past two when I went to –

The bell goes on up to twelve.

Clock's wrong. Must be an icicle in the works!

He scrabbles for his pocket watch.

Twelve! Is it noon? What has happened to the sun! I... I can't have slept through a whole day and into another night!

The bell tolls again.

A quarter past! What did Marley say?

Half-past.

Expect the first spirit...

Quarter-to.

When the clock strikes one!

The hour sounds. SCROOGE *sighs with relief.*

The hour and nothing more!

But the hour rolls on, a deep, dull, hollow, melancholy ONE. The bed curtain is drawn aside as if by magic – and the room is suddenly ablaze with pure, snow-white light.

And there's a face right by SCROOGE's. *He starts in terror.*

But the apparition is more strange than terrifying.

Androgynous, with long white hair and a smooth, youthful face, it's dressed in a simple white tunic, trimmed with summer flowers.

In one hand it carries a sprig of fresh holly and it has a huge candle-snuffer under its other arm. From its head streams a jet of dazzling white light. It is the GHOST OF CHRISTMAS PAST.

SCROOGE *gapes at it.*

Are you the spirit… whose coming was foretold to me?

GHOST OF CHRISTMAS PAST. I am!

SCROOGE. Who… what are you?

GHOST OF CHRISTMAS PAST. I am the Ghost of Christmas Past.

SCROOGE. Long past?

GHOST OF CHRISTMAS PAST. No. Your past.

SCROOGE. I see.

(*Squints.*) Would you… would you mind just putting on that cap of yours? I cannot quite –

GHOST OF CHRISTMAS PAST. What! Would you so soon put out, with worldly hands, this wonderful light I give? Is it not enough that you, Ebenezer Scrooge, are one of those whose efforts made this cap. And force me through whole trains of years to wear it low upon my brow!

SCROOGE. I meant no offence, spirit! And I can't recall having had any involvement in your bonneting –

The light surges brighter still.

What… what business brings you here?

GHOST OF CHRISTMAS PAST. Your welfare.

SCROOGE. Can't help thinking that a good night's sleep would be better for me than –

GHOST OF CHRISTMAS PAST. Your reclamation, then!

SCROOGE. Reclamation? Hmmph! I'm not a tract of Dutch fen!

The GHOST *grasps him firmly by the arm.*

GHOST OF CHRISTMAS PAST. Rise! And walk with me!

SCROOGE. I'm not properly attired, spirit, and… did I mention I have a cold in the head? And –

They are heading inexorably towards the window.

I am mortal and liable to fall!

The GHOST *puts its hand to* SCROOGE*'s heart.*

GHOST OF CHRISTMAS PAST. Bear but a touch of my hand *there* and you shall be upheld in more than this!

And they suddenly rise into the air, racing towards the wall.

SCROOGE *cries out in terror…*

SCROOGE. Good heavens!

Scene Two

SCROOGE *suddenly finds that he and the* GHOST *are standing on an open country road. It's a gorgeous, cold, winter day. Snow covers the land.*

SCROOGE *gasps.*

GHOST OF CHRISTMAS PAST. You know this place?

SCROOGE. Know it! I could walk it blindfold! I was bred here. I was a boy here!

His voice catches. He seems a little overwhelmed.

GHOST OF CHRISTMAS PAST. Your lip is trembling and… what is that upon your cheek?

SCROOGE (*snarling*). Nothing! A pimple…

SCROOGE *scowls and brushes away a tear.*

(*Asserting himself.*) Well, if you have business with me, press on, let's be done with it.

Sleigh bells sound and a bunch of young SCHOOLBOYS *dash past, laughing and chattering and full of Christmas cheer.*

SCROOGE *seems invigorated.*

Why! There's Will Scorridge! Just as I remember him! He was a funny little fellow was Will, could never sit still. They always said he had ants in his britches – And Dan – haha! Dan something or other. What was his name? I liked him. Always hoped we'd be friends but…

They must be going home. Home for the… Christmas holidays. Dan? Dan!!

He approaches one of the BOYS *but he doesn't respond.* SCROOGE *looks at the* GHOST *in puzzlement.*

GHOST OF CHRISTMAS PAST. These are but shadows of the things that have been. They have no consciousness of us.

And one BOY *in the fields hurls a snowball. It passes right through* SCROOGE.

SCROOGE (*disappointed*). Oh…

…For the best, I'm sure. What would I say to them after all these years…?

They are suddenly in front of a rather shabby school building.

GHOST OF CHRISTMAS PAST. The school is not quite deserted. A solitary child, neglected by his friends, is left there still…

SCROOGE. Yes. Yes, I know.

The light from the GHOST*'s head flares up and they are suddenly inside…*

Scene Three

…a grim, cold school-room. There are rows of empty desks at one of which sits a melancholy boy, reading a book.

SCROOGE *stares at his young self.*

SCROOGE. You are mistaken, spirit. I wasn't quite friendless.

(*Points at the book.*) There's Ali Baba! And the Sultan's groom, turned upside down by the Genii!

He gazes fondly at the gaily illustrated pages – which come to life around him. A cavalcade of colourful figures, like a panto walk-down.

Serve him right. What business had he to be married to the Princess? And there's Robin Hood! And Robinson Crusoe! And the parrot. Green body and yellow tail with a thing like lettuce growing out of the top of his head! Robinson Crusoe.

(*Regretfully, to himself.*) Where… where have you been, Robinson Crusoe?

Poor boy.

He sits down on a bench and sighs heavily. He looks at his young self and his eyes brim with tears.

(*Dries his eyes.*) I wish… No, no. It's too late now.

GHOST OF CHRISTMAS PAST. What is the matter?

SCROOGE. Nothing. Nothing. There was a boy singing a
Christmas carol at my door last night. I should like to have
given him something. That's all...

GHOST OF CHRISTMAS PAST. You did give him something.
A steel rule across the back.

*SCROOGE turns away, ashamed. The GHOST smiles a
little.*

Let us see another Christmas.

*The light flares up. Like time-lapse, the wall panels splinter
and shrink, the windows grow more cracked and dirty.*

*And the younger SCROOGE grows older. He's been joined
by his pretty little sister FAN –*

FAN. Ebenenzer!

YOUNG SCROOGE. Fan!

SCROOGE. Fan!

*...and they're standing before a dusty-looking headmaster
MR THRUMPHULL.*

*He grips the lapels of his gown in proper paterfamilias fashion,
except for when occasionally smoothing down his cow-lick of
greasy black hair or spinning the globe on his desk.*

THRUMPHULL. So! Home for the jolly holidays at last, eh,
Master Scrooge?

YOUNG SCROOGE. Yes, sir.

THRUMPHULL. Was beginnin' to think you'd be stalking
these here corridors till the last trump, eh, eh? A young buck
like you has prospects! He must travel! How I wish I'd
travelled.

He spins the globe.

Trichinopoly! By thunder, there's a name to conjure with. Or
the sultry shores of Lake Titicaca! What I wouldn't give to
be in those top-boots of yourn, young sir!

Care for some cake? Made it meself.

He offers them some unappetising cake and pale wine.

FAN (*sotto*). It's not just for the holidays, dear brother. Father is so much kinder than he used to be that home is like heaven! You're to be a man, Ebenezer, and never come back to this dreadful place!

THRUMPHULL *spins the globe again.*

THRUMPHULL. Ah, the frozen wilds of the Ross Ice Shelf!

A POSTBOY *comes in.*

Ah! There you are! You have Master Scrooge's box?

POSTBOY. Yes, Mr Thrumphull.

THRUMPHULL (*to the* POSTBOY). Care for some cake, boy? Wine? Made it meself.

POSTBOY. Is it the same grog as last year, sir?

THRUMPHULL. It is.

POSTBOY. Then, begging your pardon, sir, but I'd just as soon not.

THRUMPHULL. Hummph.

(*To* YOUNG SCROOGE.) Well now, Master Scrooge. All my best wishes and… a merry Christmas, eh, eh? Wherever you pitch up…

He shakes YOUNG SCROOGE *violently by the hand.*

YOUNG SCROOGE. Thank you, sir. Goodbye, sir.

He and FAN *race from the room, laughing.* THRUMPHULL *is left gazing at the globe.*

THRUMPHULL. Oh! Sumatra! Su-ma-tra. How it rolls off the tongue like an over-ripe Seville orange… Oh! Seville…!

Outside the school, SCROOGE *and the* GHOST *watch as* YOUNG SCROOGE *and* FAN *pause to talk.*

GHOST OF CHRISTMAS PAST. Always a delicate creature, whom a breath might have withered. But she had a large heart!

SCROOGE. So she had. You're right, I will not deny it, Spirit. God forbid!

GHOST OF CHRISTMAS PAST. She died a woman and had, as I think, children.

SCROOGE. One child.

GHOST OF CHRISTMAS PAST. True. Your...

SCROOGE. My nephew. Yes.

We're suddenly aware of the children's voices.

YOUNG SCROOGE. What's all this, Fan? Secrets? What have you and Father been plotting?

FAN. You're to be 'prenticed, brother. 'Prenticed in the City to such a dear man. Name of –

Scene Four

A forest of dark-etched warehouse offices spring up.

SCROOGE *finds himself looking up at a funny-looking old man in a Welch wig who sits at an incredibly high desk. The desk, indeed, that* SCROOGE *will one day use.*

SCROOGE. Fezziwig! Bless his heart, it's old Fezziwig alive again!

The clock on the wall is almost at seven. FEZZIWIG *consults his watch and then chuckles, a big, fat oily laugh that makes him shake all over.*

FEZZIWIG. Yo ho, there! Ebenezer! Yo ho, Jacob!

YOUNG SCROOGE, now a boy of nineteen or so, enters, grinning all over his face.

YOUNG SCROOGE. Yo ho!

With him is YOUNG MARLEY, *at this stage a serious-looking lad of the same age.*

YOUNG MARLEY *(without enthusiasm)*. Yo ho.

SCROOGE. Jacob Marley, to be sure! Bless me, yes. There he is. I had quite forgotten he was ever young!

FEZZIWIG. Yo ho, my boys! No more work tonight. Christmas Eve, Jacob! Christmas, Ebenezer! Let's have the shutters up before a man can say Jack Robinson!

YOUNG MARLEY and YOUNG SCROOGE scurry about the warehouse, putting up the shutters.

Hilli-ho! Clear away, my lads, and let's have lots of room here! Hilli-ho, Jacob! Chirrup, Ebenezer!

A thin FIDDLER enters.

My dear fellow! Up here if you please!

The FIDDLER climbs up onto FEZZIWIG's high desk, and starts tuning up his violin.

The room is all aglow.

YOUNG SCROOGE *rushes back inside.*

YOUNG MARLEY. She's here, sir.

YOUNG SCROOGE. They're all here!

And in a great rush, MRS FEZZIWIG *and her* DAUGHTERS *surge inside.*

FEZZIWIG. Here! Of course they're here! How could we have a Christmas Ball without 'em?

He embraces his wife and children. More revellers enter behind them, among them a jolly man MR BOUNCER and a pretty girl, BELLE. The FIDDLER strikes up a tune.

Oh! My dear! The Sir Roger De Coverly! May I crave…?

MRS FEZZIWIG. Well, I shall throttle you with your own shirt-front if you don't, husband!

MR BOUNCER. Quickly, sir, quickly, or I shall have the lady from under you!

And they plunge into joyful dancing. Wild shouting, hysterical laughing, flushed faces, the rum punch and port wine flowing freely.

SCROOGE *has abandoned himself to the party. Cackling, yelling, exhausting himself as he tries to join in the dancing.*

Quite well, Mr F?

A spinning FEZZIWIG *comes crashing to ground, laughing his head off.* MR BOUNCER *helps him to his feet.*

FEZZIWIG. Yes, oh yes! How's the Negus?

MR BOUNCER. Capital, as ever! And the pigeon pie fit for an Emperor. Gad, Mr F! What larks! A proper Father Christmas you are.

The GHOST *is observing with a wry smile.*

GHOST OF CHRISTMAS PAST. A small matter to make these silly folks so full of gratitude.

SCROOGE. Small!

GHOST OF CHRISTMAS PAST. Why! Is it not? He has spent but a few pounds of your mortal money: three or four perhaps. Is that so much that he deserves this praise?

SCROOGE. It isn't that. He has the power to render us happy or unhappy. To make our service light or burdensome – a pleasure or a toil. The happiness he gives is quite as great as if it cost… cost a… fortune.

GHOST OF CHRISTMAS PAST. What is the matter?

SCROOGE. Nothing particular.

GHOST OF CHRISTMAS PAST. Something, I think?

SCROOGE. No. I should like to be able to say a word or two to my clerk just now! That's all.

He's suddenly alert. He's noticed something.

YOUNG SCROOGE *is standing stock still, rooted by the sight of* BELLE. *She is talking with friends then suddenly looks up as though aware she's being watched.*

BELLE *catches* YOUNG SCROOGE's *eye, smiles.*

He smiles back.

Belle. Oh my sweet Belle. Yes… it *was* that Christmas.

YOUNG SCROOGE *moves towards her, then is distracted by the sight of* YOUNG MARLEY, *slipping into his coat and hat.*

YOUNG SCROOGE. What? Going so soon, Jacob?

YOUNG MARLEY (*shushing him*). Time and tide, Ebenezer. Time and tide. Not a word to old Fezziwig, but I have a a… financial speculation of my own to attend to. And ain't it ripenin' nicely!

YOUNG SCROOGE. But Jacob! On Christmas Eve!

YOUNG MARLEY. Christmas be hanged! Business don't take a holiday, Ebenezer. You'd be wise to remember that.

(*Thinks.*) In fact, why not come in with me on it? You have a few bob put by, don't you? I've seen you counting it.

YOUNG SCROOGE. Yes. Against the day.

YOUNG MARLEY. What do you mean?

YOUNG SCROOGE. The day that I marry. Raise a family.

YOUNG MARLEY *scoffs. Then gazes into the distance, wistfully.*

YOUNG MARLEY. There's a chill in the air, my friend.

YOUNG SCROOGE. Aye, they say the Thames'll freeze again –

YOUNG MARLEY (*harsh laugh*). 'Tis the chill wind of pecuniary reality I speak of. We will soon live in a world of smoke and manufactories, Ebenezer, of slog and sweat. 'Fraid old Fezziwig's one of a dying breed. We must look to the future if we're to survive. What do you say? There's still time to invest. This little venture of mine...

YOUNG SCROOGE (*thoughtful*). Maybe you're right, Jacob. But I've an eye on a different sort of future tonight.

He looks towards BELLE.

YOUNG MARLEY. Ha, ha! Well, all luck to you, my friend. But think about what I've said.

YOUNG SCROOGE. I shall.

YOUNG MARLEY's words do seem to have impacted upon him.

I shall.

MARLEY *turns to go.*

A merry Christmas, Jacob!

YOUNG MARLEY (*looks him up and down*). Hmmph.

He goes out into the snow. SCROOGE *looks thoughtful, then turns towards* BELLE, *his face wreathed in smiles. He goes towards her and bows.*

YOUNG SCROOGE. Would you like to –

BELLE (*eager*). Yes!

They dance slowly together. Something wonderful is beginning...

GHOST OF CHRISTMAS PAST. My time grows short! Come!

Scene Five

The white light flares up again and the dancing figures of
YOUNG SCROOGE *and* BELLE *become... a little older and
well-dressed.*

*They're in the same warehouse, now noticeably more austere-
looking.*

YOUNG SCROOGE. What is this all about?

BELLE. It doesn't matter.

YOUNG SCROOGE. Indeed? I think it matters a great deal!
There's no one else, if that's what you're thinking!

BELLE. Of course not. I know that, Ebenezer. Not someone
else. Some*thing*. I have been displaced. By an idol.

YOUNG SCROOGE. An idol?

BELLE. A golden one.

YOUNG SCROOGE (*harsh laugh*). Oh I see! This is the even-
handed dealing of the world! There's nothing on which it is
so hard as poverty and there is nothing it professes to
condemn with such severity as the pursuit of wealth!

BELLE. You fear the world too much! Remember all those
hopes? All those beautiful dreams? The dreams we had
together. Replaced by this... obsession.

YOUNG SCROOGE. Obsession?

BELLE. With money! Money above all things!

YOUNG SCROOGE. I have grown *up,* Belle. That's all. But...
but none of that changes my feelings for you.

BELLE. Our engagement is an old one. We did it when we were
both poor and content to be so. You *are* changed. When it
was made, you were another man.

YOUNG SCROOGE. I was a boy. Have I ever sought release
from you?

BELLE. In words. No. Never.

She tries to touch his cheek but he pulls away. He wants answers.

YOUNG SCROOGE. In what, then?

BELLE. In a changed nature. In an altered spirit. In everything that made my love of any worth or value in your sight. If this had never been between us...

She holds out her hand. A plain gold ring shines on her finger.

...tell me, would you seek me out and try to win me now?

YOUNG SCROOGE. Of... of course!

BELLE. I wish I could believe you, Ebenezer. But the man you have become would never marry a penniless girl. I release you, with a full heart, for the love of him you once were.

YOUNG SCROOGE. Belle!

BELLE (*sobs and pulls off the ring*). May you be happy in the life you have chosen!

She rushes out of the office. SCROOGE *picks up the ring and goes after her. He comes upon* WORKMEN *replacing* FEZZIWIG's *business sign with a new one.* YOUNG MARLEY, *also looking prosperous, stops them as they work.*

YOUNG MARLEY. Wait!

The WORKMEN *rotate the sign. It bears the legend 'SCROOGE and MARLEY'.*

Has a ring to it, eh?

YOUNG SCROOGE. Should have been your name first, Jacob.

YOUNG MARLEY (*darkly humorous*). An act of generosity for an old friend. Won't happen again!

He nods towards BELLE's *retreating figure.*

Trouble?

YOUNG SCROOGE. No. No trouble. Just… just a silly dream.

YOUNG MARLEY. No profit in dreams, Ebenezer.

He goes. SCROOGE *examines the ring.*

YOUNG SCROOGE. (*to the* WORKMAN). You there! Boy!

He tosses the ring to the WORKMAN.

Take that to Screbbitt's on Monmouth Street. See what you can get for it.

He follows MARLEY *off.*

And we find the older SCROOGE *looking to where* BELLE *disappeared.*

SCROOGE. Oh Belle. My sweet Belle…

GHOST OF CHRISTMAS PAST. You wish to see her again?

SCROOGE. I do!

GHOST OF CHRISTMAS PAST. Then let us see one shade more!

The white light flares again.

Scene Six

A lady – an older BELLE *– is sitting by the fire in a charming, comfortable home.*

CHILDREN *are running riot, examining presents and helping their* FATHER *to dress the Christmas tree.*

FATHER. I saw an old friend of yours this afternoon, my dear.

BELLE. Who?

FATHER. Guess!

BELLE. How can I? Oh, I don't I know. How can I guess?

FATHER. Guess!

He hunches over in a miserly pose.

BELLE. Mr Scrooge?

FATHER. Mr Scrooge it was! I passed his office window and as it was not shut up, and he had a candle inside, I could scarcely help seeing him there, with that miserly partner of his. Two peas in a pod those two! Two peas in a pod!

BELLE looks sad for a moment. Then one of the CHILDREN bounces towards her.

CHILD. Look, Mama! Look what Elspeth has done to my dolly-dalkin!

SCROOGE. Spirit! Remove me from this place. Why do you delight to torture me?

GHOST OF CHRISTMAS PAST. I told you these were shadows of the things that have been. That they are what they are, do not blame me!

SCROOGE. Remove me! I cannot bear it!

He turns to the GHOST and wrestles the great extinguisher cap from the GHOST.

It's like trying to close the lid on a furnace but slowly he manages to force the cap onto the column of white light. The GHOST diminishes beneath it but the white light floods out from beneath the cap.

SCROOGE gives one more heave and there's only darkness.

He looks about and realises he's back in his bedroom. Then, overcome by exhaustion he swoons, falls onto his bed and is asleep upon the instant.

NARRATOR. Scrooge awoke in the middle of a prodigious snore…

SCROOGE is snoring loudly and wakes with a start.

He looks about in a panic, then freezes as he hears the church clock striking the quarters again.

SCROOGE. Another night! Another night has passed. And I'm
to expect the *second* spirit on the stroke of one. P'raps it
won't come. Yes, that's it. They'll see I've learned my
lesson. Oh yes.

The clock strikes one.

And reddish light blazes out from beneath the bedroom door.
SCROOGE *gasps – but then nothing more happens.*

Hello?

Still the light pours in but no apparition appears.

NARRATOR. Scrooge was ready for a good broad field of
strange appearances. Nothing between a baby and a
rhinoceros would have astonished him very much.

But, being prepared for almost anything, he was not by any
means prepared for nothing...

The light blazes on. Nothing more.

SCROOGE. It's worse not knowing than confronting the brute.
Whatever it is.

He gets out of bed and puts his hand on the doorknob.
Suddenly, a thunderous voice!

GHOST OF CHRISTMAS PRESENT. *EBENEZER*
SCROOGE! Come in! Come in!

The bedroom becomes the parlour – but it's utterly
transformed.

Holly, ivy, mistletoe hang everywhere glistening in the light
from the roaring fire.

A 'throne' has been formed from turkeys, geese, suckling-
pigs, sausage-strings, mince pies, plum puddings, barrels of
oysters, oranges, luscious pears.

Seething bowls of punch make the room dim with their
delicious steam.

On the 'throne' sits the GHOST OF CHRISTMAS
PRESENT: *a giant – robed in green, his chest bare and a
wreath of icicle-hung holly encircling his brow.*

Come in! And know me better, man!!

Interval.

ACT THREE

Scene One

THE GHOST OF CHRISTMAS PRESENT *as before on his throne of food and goodies. There's something delightfully boozy and Falstaffian about the* GHOST*'s ruddy face, but there's an edge to him too, a manic, carnal glint in the eye that speaks more of the Pagan Green Man than of Santa Claus...*

SCROOGE *edges his way in. The* GHOST *raises a blazing torch, like a Horn of Plenty.*

GHOST OF CHRISTMAS PRESENT. You have never seen the likes of me before!

SCROOGE. Never!

GHOST OF CHRISTMAS PRESENT. I am the Ghost of Christmas Present.

SCROOGE. I guessed as much.

The GHOST *downs a huge goblet of wine. Most of it spills down his beard and chest.*

GHOST OF CHRISTMAS PRESENT. And yet you have not walked abroad with any of my brothers, my elder brothers, have you, you weird little man?

SCROOGE. How... how many brothers do you have?

GHOST OF CHRISTMAS PRESENT. More than eighteen hundred!

SCROOGE. A tremendous family to provide for! I suppose you must have independent means –

The GHOST *silences him with a glare. Then laughs heartily and stuffs pie into his mouth.*

SCROOGE. Spirit, conduct me where you will. I went forth last night on compulsion and I learnt a lesson which is… working now. Tonight, if you have aught to teach me, let me profit by it.

GHOST OF CHRISTMAS PRESENT. Touch my robe.

SCROOGE *does so and the room changes…*

Scene Two

A beautiful, crisp Christmas morning. The shops are all opening up and it's a riot of colour and noise. French plums and fresh coffee and Spanish onions and puddings galore.

Snow is being scraped away from doorways and families are making their happy way to church. Bells peal madly and everywhere people are wishing each other 'a merry Christmas'.

The GHOST – *colossally tall* – *sprinkles droplets of moisture from his torch onto all of them.* SCROOGE *looks on, intrigued.*

An aproned WAITER *rushes from a baker's shop to his restaurant and almost collides with a* SECOND WAITER.

WAITER. Mind yesself, you great useless article, afore I horse-whip ya!

SECOND WAITER. H'I should like to see you try! H'Ive 'ad ha bellyful of your threats to hassassinate me!

They come face to face, blazing with anger. The GHOST *drifts past and sprinkles more droplets on them.*

WAITER (*beaming*). Mind you, on account of the day, it seems out of keeping to –

SECOND WAITER. Quite right, 'arry, my lad. A merry Christmas to you and yours!

WAITER. And to you, I'm sure.

SCROOGE *hurries to catch up with the* GHOST. *In a blur, he sees Christmas dinners being prepared in house after house.*

SCROOGE. Is there a peculiar flavour in what you sprinkle from your torch?

GHOST OF CHRISTMAS PRESENT. There is. My own.

SCROOGE. Would it apply to any kind of dinner on this day?

GHOST OF CHRISTMAS PAST. To any kindly given. To a poor one most.

SCROOGE. Why to a poor one most?

GHOST OF CHRISTMAS PAST. Because it needs it most.

Scene Three

They're suddenly inside a tiny but cheerful house. The GHOST, *despite its size, fits in beneath the rotting rafters.*

MRS CRATCHIT *is laying the table. Her pretty face is tired and her clothes patched and often mended.* BELINDA CRATCHIT *is smoothing down the cloth.* PETER CRATCHIT *is picking at a pan of vegetables.*

It's a familiar and universal scene. The bustling, stressful family home on Christmas Day.

MRS CRATCHIT. Mind, Peter! Get out from under my skirts, will you?

PETER. Sorry, Mum.

MRS CRATCHIT. As if I didn't have enough to do. And leave them 'taters alone!

She cuffs him round the ear.

What do you think you look like?

Young PETER *rises from the pan. He's wearing one of his father's collars and is swamped by it.*

PETER (*mouth full*). A proper swell, that's what! Going strolling in the Vauxhall gardens and that with my lady love.

MRS CRATCHIT. Well, you'll ruin your dad's best collar and I'll be the one that has to launder it.

She smoothes his hair from his eyes and looks him fondly up and down.

No lady'll have you with your mouth full of 'taters!

Two more CRATCHITS – EDWIN *and* GRACE – *race in.*

EDWIN. Is the goose cooked, Ma?

GRACE. We was outside the baker's looking at the candies. And there was oranges and lemons like cricket balls and –

EDWIN. And then we smelt the goose and we knew it was ours.

PETER. The great Cratchit goose, of Camden Town. It's a legend!

BELINDA. Is them 'taters done, Peter?

PETER (*winks*). What's left of 'em.

MRS CRATCHIT. Dunno what's keeping your father. And Tim. And Martha weren't as late last Christmas Day by half-an-hour.

The door opens, revealing MARTHA.

MARTHA. Here's Martha, Mother!

BELINDA. Here she is!

EDWIN. Wait till you see the goose, Martha!

MRS CRATCHIT. How late you are, love!

MARTHA. Well, we'd a deal of work to finish up last night and had to clear away this morning, Mum.

MRS CRATCHIT. Well. Never mind so long as you are come. Sit down before the fire, love, and have a warm, bless you.

From off we hear 'Hear we come a wassailing'…

BOB *and* TIM (*voice-over, singing*). 'God bless you and send you a happy new year…'

GRACE. No, no. There's Dad coming. Hide, Martha!

EDWIN. Hide!

BELINDA. Table!

MARTHA runs to hide under the table. In comes BOB CRATCHIT, *accompanied by his son* TIM.

BOB *and* TIM (*ending the song*). '…and God send you a Happy New Year!'

They bow extravagantly to the family.

Pale and hollow eyed, TINY TIM *has a crutch. He limps over to his usual place by the fire.*

BOB. Where's Martha?

MRS CRATCHIT. Not coming.

BOB (*genuinely downcast*). Not coming! Not coming on Christmas Day?

MRS CRATCHIT. I know! Ain't it a shame!

PETER. Awful shame!

EDWIN. Fearful shame!

MARTHA. Oh, I can't bear it, Dad! Even if it's only for a joke. Here I am!

She comes flying out from under the table and BOB *embraces her. He kisses all his children.*

PETER *and* BELINDA *help* TIM *to the kitchen.*

EDWIN. Come and hear the pudding in the copper, Tim!

GRACE. Singing like archangels, it is!

TINY TIM. Cor!

BOB and MRS CRATCHIT *watch him go.*

MRS CRATCHIT. How was he today, love?

BOB. Good as gold. And better. Somehow he gets thoughtful sitting by himself so much, and thinks the strangest things you ever heard. He told me, coming home, that he hoped the people saw him in the church, because of how he is, and it might be pleasant to them to remember upon Christmas Day, who made the lame walk, and blind men see...

His voice cracks a little and MRS CRATCHIT *squeezes his hand.*

He's getting stronger, my love. I know he is. He'll grow hale and hearty.

But he can't meet his wife's gaze. MARTHA, *too, busies herself.*

Now! Where's that punch?

TINY TIM, EDWIN *and* GRACE *scramble back into the kitchen as* BOB *prepares the gin-punch.* TINY TIM *has settled down into his accustomed place on a stool by the fire.* SCROOGE *looks over sadly at him.*

MRS CRATCHIT. Oh God! The goose!

But PETER *parades into the kitchen with the Christmas goose on a platter.*

BOB *sweeps up* TINY TIM *and deposits him at the table where the others are already waiting, banging their cutlery on the table.*

MRS CRATCHIT *carves the goose and steaming stuffing pours out.*

BOB *swallows the first, blessed mouthful, eyes closed.*

BOB. Oh! Oh my dears! Such a goose! There never was such a goose!

And the family fall upon their food.

Time passes in a blur. Flushed faces, happy smiles. MRS CRATCHIT *mildly burping.*

PETER. Pudding! It's pudding time!

BELINDA. Don't think I've room!

EDWIN. I'll have yours then!

They laugh. PETER *goes off to the outhouse to fetch the pudding.*

MRS CRATCHIT. I feel quite faint. What if it ain't done enough? I confess –

She draws MARTHA *nearer to her.*

– I has my doubts about the quantity of flour…

MARTHA. Don't be daft.

TINY TIM. It'll be right as ninepence. When is it ever not, eh, Dad?

BOB. Never in all these Christmases has it been less than superlative, my love.

MRS CRATCHIT. But what if it breaks when we turn it out?

TINY TIM (*mock serious*). What if burglars has got over the wall and had it away with it while we were merry with the goose?

MRS CRATCHIT (*chuckling*). Oh, you're awful. You're all awful.

But here it comes! PETER *brings it in a like the Crown Jewels. A little black canon-ball of a pudding, ablaze with blue fire.*

BOB. She's surpassed herself again, ain't she, my dears! This pudding…

He hooks his thumbs into the lapels of his waistcoat like an Alderman.

…THIS pudding I hereby declare the crowning glory of my dear wife's marital career!

MARTHA. Hear, hear!

BOB. Now I've waited till this day of all days to impart a little information. It's what we in the world of high finance –

MRS CRATCHIT *giggles.*

Sauce. It's what we Captains of Industry refers to as a opportunity. I have my eye on a situation for Master Peter Cratchit over yonder – him as is drowning in his dad's Sunday best collar and has got his father's looks besides – a situation that will bring in, if obtained, full five and six weekly!

TINY TIM. Five and six!

MARTHA. Peter!

PETER. Blimey!

BOB. Now warn't that worth saving up?

BOB *raises a chipped custard mug full of punch.*

A merry Christmas to us all, my dears. God bless us.

ALL. God bless us!

TINY TIM. God bless us, every one!

BOB *reaches down and holds his son's hand. He smiles bravely.*

SCROOGE *turns to the* GHOST.

SCROOGE. Spirit, tell me if Tiny Tim will live.

GHOST OF CHRISTMAS PRESENT. I see a vacant seat in the poor chimney-corner and a crutch without an owner, carefully preserved. If these shadows remain unaltered by the Future none other of my race will find him here.

SCROOGE. No, no! Oh no, kind Spirit. Say he will be spared!

GHOST OF CHRISTMAS PRESENT. What then? If he be like to die, he had better do it, *and decrease the surplus population!*

SCROOGE *hangs his head in shame. The* GHOST *looms massively, terrifyingly over him.*

Who are *you* to decide what men shall live, what men shall die? It may be, that in the sight of Heaven, you are more worthless and less fit to live than millions like this poor man's child. Oh God! To hear the insect on the leaf pronouncing on the *excess of life* among his hungry brothers in the dust!

SCROOGE *cowers, sobbing before the* GHOST*'s wrath.*

BOB (*offstage*). Mr Scrooge!

SCROOGE. Eh? What?

SCROOGE *looks up.*

BOB. I'll give you Mr Scrooge, the Founder of the Feast!

But the family don't raise their glasses.

MRS CRATCHIT. The Founder of the Feast indeed! I wish I had him here. I'd give him a piece of my mind to feast upon, and I hope he'd have a good appetite for it.

BOB. My dear, the children. Christmas Day.

MRS CRATCHIT. It should be Christmas Day, I am sure, on which one drinks the health of such an odious, stingy, hard, unfeeling man as Mr Scrooge. You know he is, Robert. Nobody knows it better than you do, poor fellow.

BOB (*mildly*). My dear. Christmas Day.

MRS CRATCHIT. I'll drink his health for your sake and the Day's, not for his. Long life to him. A merry Christmas and a happy new year!

He'll be very merry and very happy, I have no doubt!

ALL (*without enthusiasm*). Mr Scrooge...

SCROOGE. Oh! Very gratifying, I'm sure. Did you hear that – ?

He attempts a weak smile but the GHOST *merely glares at him.*

SCROOGE *notices something. A bulky shape in the folds of the* GHOST*'s mantle down about his ankles. But he looks away at the sound of the* CRATCHITS *lustily singing 'Here we go a-wassailing', their eyes bright and shining,* TINY TIM*'s most of all.*

Scene Four

SCROOGE *and the* GHOST *are suddenly on a bleak and blasted moor, dotted about with great rocks.*

SCROOGE. What is this place?

GHOST OF CHRISTMAS PRESENT. A place where miners live, who labour in the bowels of the earth. But they know me. See!

A very old MINER *sits in a place of honour in a threadbare chair, singing a plaintive and beautiful old Christmas carol.*

Suddenly a great black wave rises up, threatening to crash over them! SCROOGE *reacts in terror.*

But then he and the GHOST *are hovering over a wild, stormy sea, black as night. They circle a lighthouse and two* KEEPERS *are visible through the snow-streaked window –*

KEEPER 1. 'Though three men dwell on Flannan Isle, to keep the lamp alight. As we steered under the lee, we caught no glimmer through the night!' Haha. Compliments of the season, Jeremiah!

KEEPER 2. And the same to you, old pal!

Toasting and laughing – and now a mass of frozen rigging looms through the fog and they're swooping over a ship.

The HELMSMAN *at the ship's wheel gratefully accepts a mug of grog from a* SEAMAN.

HELMSMAN. Bless you, Albert. And don't you fret none about the watch. I'll see to it.

SEAMAN. 'Tain't necessary, sir! 'Tis my watch.

HELMSMAN. Aye, and you'll be needing your sleep if you're to be fresh and handsome for your missus when we dock! Now away to your bunk with you.

SEAMAN (*beaming*). Bless you, sir. Merry Christmas!

HELMSMAN. Merry Christmas, my boy.

The HELMSMAN *smiles contentedly to himself.*

The scene darkens and we hear –

FRED (*voice-over*). He said that Christmas was a humbug, as I live! He believed it too.

Scene Five

A room blazing with light!

SCROOGE's *nephew* FRED *is laughing his head off.*

CAROLINE. More shame for him, Fred.

The room is crowded with PARTY GUESTS. *There's a very relaxed air.* FRED's *friend* TOPPER *laughs.*

TOPPER. He sounds a comical old fellow.

FRED. He's not as pleasant as he might be, but his offences carry their own punishment and I have nothing to say against him!

CAROLINE. I'm sure he's very rich, Fred. At least you always tell me so.

FRED. What of that, my dear? His wealth is of no use to him. He don't do any good with it. He don't make himself comfortable with it.

(*Laughing.*) He hasn't the satisfaction of thinking that he is ever going to benefit us with it.

CAROLINE. I have no patience with him.

The other ladies murmur their agreement.

FRED. Oh, I'm sorry for him! I couldn't be angry with him if I tried. Who suffers by his ill whims? Himself, always. Here, he takes it into his head to dislike us, and he won't come and dine with us. What's the consequence? He don't lose much of a dinner.

CAROLINE (*mock indignation*). Indeed, I think he loses a very good dinner!

ALL. Hear, hear!

FRED. Well. I'm very glad to hear it, because I haven't great faith in these young housekeepers. What do you say, Topper?

TOPPER *pulls a dejected face and looks sideways at a pretty lady called* POLL.

TOPPER. I ain't got the right to express an opinion, Fred. Since I'm a wretched bachelor and, therefore, no better than an outcast!

POLL *blushes and bats at him with her fan. He smiles slyly.*

FRED. Anyway, all I'll say is that by not making merry with us, my uncle loses a few pleasant moments – pleasanter than he can find in his mouldy old office or his dusty chambers – and I mean to give him the same chance every year whether he likes it or not!

A polka strikes up.

CAROLINE. Oh!

FRED *sweeps her up and into the dance.*

SCROOGE. Mercy, I remember this one!

TOPPER. Who's there? Who?

He glances at the GHOST. *It's suddenly perceptibly older-looking.* SCROOGE *doesn't seem to notice as he's too caught up in the fun.*

The GHOST *looks down greedily at the table and begins shovelling food and wine into his mouth.*

TOPPER, *blindfolded, is now playing at Blind Man's Buff.*

He's pursuing POLL *across the room.*

CAROLINE. Outrageous!

Everyone's laughing heartily. TOPPER *gropes at* FRED*'s waist.*

TOPPER. No, no. Too thick. That can't be –

Laughing, POLL *hides behind the curtains – and* TOPPER *heads straight for her.*

FRED. How does he do it? With the resolution of an eighty-gunner, Mr Topper sails towards the object of his affections!

CAROLINE. Fred, you've cooked this up between you!

FRED. Oh shush!

TOPPER *suddenly lunges for* POLL *and grabs her round the waist.*

She pulls the blindfold off him.

TOPPER. Oh my! Miss Polly! It's you!

She giggles and pulls the curtain around them both.

POLL. Ooh, Mr Topper…

ALL. *FINALLY!!*

SCROOGE *is transformed. He's grinning like an eager little boy. Time passes in a blur.*

SCROOGE. Here's a new game! One half-hour more, Spirit, I beg!

MISS CHOAKPEAR. It's an animal, then?

FRED. Yes.

TOPPER. Fierce or friendly?

POLL. Nay, it's my turn, Mr Topper! Is it fierce?

FRED. Yes!

CAROLINE. Savage!

FRED. Yes!

MISS CHOKEPEAR. Does it live in Africa?

FRED. No.

MR CHOKEPEAR. Europe?

FRED. Yes.

SCROOGE. A bear! It's a bear! Oh…

He's saddened they cannot hear him.

MR CHOAKPEAR. A bear?

SCROOGE. Aha!

FRED. Nooo…

SCROOGE. Oh.

TOPPER. Does it live in a menagerie?

FRED. No.

CAROLINE. Not even in London?

POLL. It lives in London, then?

FRED hesitates.

FRED. Oh yes!

MR GRUB. A horse?

FRED. No.

MISS GRUB. A dog?

FRED. No!

He's giggling uncontrollably.

CAROLINE. What is it? Is it a pig?

FRED. Ha! No.

MISS GRUB. Oh! I know! I have found it out! I know what it is!

FRED. What?

MISS GRUB. It's your Uncle Scrooge!

FRED *nods and laughs.*

The company burst out laughing but the smile is wiped from SCROOGE*'s face.*

He turns away sadly.

TOPPER (*offstage*). I call foul!

CAROLINE (*offstage*). Why, Mr Topper?

TOPPER. Because Mr Chokepear there asked if it were a bear and Fred said 'no'!

They laugh again. SCROOGE *is downcast then suddenly notices the change in the* GHOST. *Its hair is snow-white and its ruddy face lined with age.*

SCROOGE. Spirit, you are... Are... are spirits' lives so short?

GHOST OF CHRISTMAS PRESENT. My life upon this globe is very brief. It ends tonight.

SCROOGE. Tonight!

GHOST OF CHRISTMAS PRESENT. Tonight at midnight. Hark! The time is drawing near!

Scene Six

They're suddenly outside. The GHOST *looks haggard and weary.* SCROOGE *looks down at the spirit's robe again.*

SCROOGE. Forgive me if I am not justified in what I ask but I see something strange, and not belonging to yourself, protruding from your skirts. Is it a foot or a claw?

GHOST OF CHRISTMAS PRESENT. It might be a claw, for the flesh there is upon it. Look here.

He unfolds his robe. Clinging to his bare ankles are a BOY *and a* GIRL. *But so wretched, wolfish, horrible are they that they scarcely seem human. Their flesh is yellow and pinched, their eyes dull, their mouths slavering maws.*

Yet they are pathetic and feeble too.

SCROOGE *gasps and falls back, appalled.*

SCROOGE. What... what delightful children... you must be very pr–

He can't go on pretending.

Spirit! Are they yours?

GHOST OF CHRISTMAS PRESENT. They are Man's! And they cling to me, appealing from their fathers. This boy is Ignorance. This girl is Want. Beware them both but most of all beware this boy!

SCROOGE. Have they no refuge or resource?

And the wretched children and the strange, feral GHOST *loom over him one last time.*

GHOST OF CHRISTMAS PRESENT. *Are there no prisons? Are there no workhouses? ARE THERE NO PRISONS? ARE THERE NO WORKHOUSES?*

The church clock strikes twelve with a tremendous percussion.

SCROOGE *looks up at the clock and when he looks back the* GHOST OF CHRISTMAS PRESENT *has vanished.*

SCROOGE *is suddenly aware that all sound seems to have leeched away, as though muffled by heavy snow. He looks around and sees…*

…drifting like a mist towards him, the dreadful, draped and hooded figure of the GHOST OF CHRISTMAS YET TO COME…

ACT FOUR

Scene One

The GHOST *is tall and stately and swathed in black cloth, the figure beneath totally unseen except for one bare, outstretched hand.*

SCROOGE *is immediately terrified by the apparition and sinks to his knees.*

SCROOGE. I am in the presence of the Ghost of Christmas Yet to Come?

The GHOST *merely inclines its head slightly.*

You are about to show me shadows of the things that have not happened, but will happen in the time before us. Is that so, Spirit?

The GHOST *responds in the same way, then begins to glide off.* SCROOGE *tries to get up but is shaking with fear and the* GHOST *appears to look back at him.*

Ghost of the future! I fear you more than any spectre I have seen. But as I know your purpose is to do me good, and as I hope to live to be another man from what I was, I am prepared to bear you company, and do it with a thankful heart. Will you not speak to me?

For answer, the GHOST *only stretches out its hand, pointing the way ahead.*

Lead on, then. Lead on. The night is waning fast, and it is precious time to me, I know. Lead on, Spirit…

And a strong shaft of sunlight passes across his face, making him squint.

Around him, buildings spring up like phantoms and light and dark change rapidly like the beating of great wings.

Scene Two

SCROOGE *and the* GHOST *are suddenly amid the bustle and chatter of the stock market exchange in the City. Sober, prosperous* MEN *are dotted about discussing business, exchanging letters and contracts and piles of money.*

The GHOST *points towards a knot of* MEN *and* SCROOGE *gingerly advances. A man,* PLUMCHUTE, *is holding court.*

PLUMCHUTE. No, I don't know much about it, either way. I only know he's dead.

GIPP. Old Scratch gone, eh! When did he die?

PLUMCHUTE. Last night, I believe.

TOTTERALL (*inhaling snuff*). Why, what was the matter with him? I thought he'd never die.

PLUMCHUTE. God knows.

GIPP. What has he done with his money?

PLUMCHUTE. I haven't heard. Left it to his company, perhaps. He hasn't left it to me. That's all I know. Ha, ha!

General laughter.

It's likely to be a very cheap funeral, for upon my life I don't know of anybody to go to it. Suppose we make up a party and volunteer?

TOTTERALL. I don't mind going if a lunch is provided, but I must be fed, if I make one.

PLUMCHUTE. Well, I am the most disinterested among you, after all, for I never wear black gloves, and I never eat lunch. But I'll offer to go, if anybody else will. When I come to think of it, I'm not at all sure that I wasn't his most particular friend; for we used to stop and exchange well... not exactly pleasantries!

More laughter. The crowd disperses.

SCROOGE (*puzzled*). They can't be speaking of old Marley, for this… this is the future.

Looks around.

And no sign of me in my usual place… But then! Naturally not! For I'm resolved to change and so –

The GHOST *is beside him and seems to be regarding him balefully. It raises its arm and the scene changes.*

Scene Three

They're suddenly in the worst part of London. The Rookery. A vile, stinking hovel reeking of crime, filth and misery.

Fearfully, SCROOGE *creeps along in the* GHOST*'s wake. The people half-visible in the shadows are half-naked, slipshod, drunken.*

They stop outside a 'shop'. It's a fearful, horrible slum.

The GHOST *bids* SCROOGE *go inside.*

On the floor are piles of rusty keys, nails, chains, mountains of rags, masses of corrupted fat, and sepulchres of bones.

OLD JOE – *the proprietor – sits amongst his wares, smoking a clay pipe. He's a twinkle-eyed villain, steeped in crime and muck. With him are a drudge of a laundress,* MRS DILBER, *and a pale young man in black,* MR THURSDAY.

OLD JOE *looks up and seems to stare at* SCROOGE, *who falters.*

MRS CHITTY. Well! If we all three haven't met 'ere without meaning it!

SCROOGE *turns to find that behind him is a charwoman* MRS CHITTY.

Charwoman, laundress and undertaker's man! Look here, old Joe, what a co-in-side-ence, eh?

OLD JOE (*cackles*). You couldn't have met in a better place than my parlour! You was made free of it long ago, you know and the other two an't strangers. Lord, how that door skreeks! There an't such a rusty bit of metal in the place as its own hinges, I believe and I'm sure there's no such old bones here, as mine. Ha, ha!

MRS DILBER *looks worried*.

MRS CHITTY. Don't stand staring as if you was afraid, woman! Who's the wiser? We're not going to pick holes in each other's coats, I suppose?

MRS DILBER. No, indeed.

MR THURSDAY. I should hope not.

MRS CHITTY. Who's the worse for the loss of a few things like these? Not a dead man, I suppose.

MRS DILBER. No, indeed!

She laughs, relaxes a bit.

MRS CHITTY. If he wanted to keep them after he was dead, the wicked old screw, why wasn't he natural in his lifetime? If he had been, he'd have had somebody to look after him when he was struck with Death, instead of lying gasping out his last there, alone by himself. So, we've all 'elped ourselves and where's the harm in that?

MR THURSDAY *advances with a bundle, then steps back*.

MR THURSDAY. Ladies first.

MRS CHITTY. We don't stand on such ceremony 'ere, eh, Joe? You go first, Mr Thursday.

He smiles a sickly smile and uncovers the bundle.

MR THURSDAY. Cufflinks, a wax seal and a pencil case.

OLD JOE. Hmmph. No gold in his teeth, I s'pose?

MR THURSDAY. Nah. I can never get that close. The Guvnor
watches me like an 'awk as it is.

OLD JOE scribbles some figures in chalk on the wall.

OLD JOE. That's your account and I wouldn't give another
sixpence, if I was to be boiled for not doing it.

MR THURSDAY. 'Ardly worth the walk!

OLD JOE. Who's next?

MRS DILBER. Me.

She flings open her bundle.

His boots, some towels. Some spoons.

OLD JOE. Hmm. And a pair of sugar tongs. Well, there's the
reckoning.

He scratches on the wall.

MRS DILBER *(appalled)*. Oh!

OLD JOE. I always give too much to ladies. It's a weakness of
mine, and that's the way I ruin myself. That's your account.
If you asked me for another penny I'd repent of being so
liberal and knock off half-a-crown.

MRS CHITTY *(proudly)*. Now undo my bundle, Joe.

*OLD JOE does so and lifts some dark, expensive-looking
material.*

OLD JOE. What do you call this?

MRS CHITTY. Bed curtains!

OLD JOE. Bed curtains! You don't mean to say you took them
down, rings and all, with him lying there?

MRS CHITTY. Yes I do. Why not?

OLD JOE *(shaking his head)*. You was born to make your
fortune and you'll certainly do it.

He lifts a lamp to examine them.

MRS CHITTY. Don't drop that oil upon the blankets, now!

OLD JOE. *His* blankets?

MRS CHITTY. Whose else's do you think? He isn't likely to take cold without them, I dare say.

OLD JOE *suddenly drops the blankets.*

OLD JOE. 'Ere! He didn't die of anything catching, did he?!

MRS CHITTY *cackles horribly.*

MRS CHITTY. I an't so fond of his company that I'd loiter about him for such things, if he did. And you may look through that shirt till your eyes ache but you won't find a hole in it. It's the best he had, and a fine one too. They'd have wasted it, if it hadn't been for me.

OLD JOE. What do you call wasting of it?

MRS CHITTY. Putting it on him to be buried in, to be sure. Somebody was fool enough to do it, but I took it off again.

MR THURSDAY (*mournfully*). Calico's good enough for 'im! It's quite as becoming to the body.

MRS CHITTY. And he can't look uglier than he did in that one!

They all laugh shrilly.

SCROOGE *shrinks back in horror from these ghouls. He peers about for the* GHOST *which is all but invisible in the gloom.*

SCROOGE. Spirit! I see, I see. The case of this unhappy man might be my own. My life tends that way, now. Merciful Heaven, what is this?

Scene Four

SCROOGE *jumps back from touching a bed. They're now in a dark room. Pale light from a grimy window just about illuminates the stark, un-curtained bed and the sheeted figure of a corpse that lies on it.*

The GHOST *points implacably down towards the covered face of the body.*

SCROOGE. Great God, this is a dreadful place! In... in leaving it, I shall not forget its lesson. Let us go!

But the GHOST *doesn't move.*

I know what you intend! This poor wretch might be me! If he were resurrected now, his first thoughts would be avarice... hard-dealing, griping cares! And look what a rich end such concerns have brought him to.

The GHOST *points urgently at the covered face.*

(*Sobs.*) I understand you and I would do it, if I could. But I have not the power, Spirit. I have not the power!... If there is any person in the town, who feels emotion caused by this man's death, show that person to me, Spirit, I beseech you.

The GHOST *seems to consider, then raises its robed arm like a wing...*

Scene Five

A poor but decent home. A woman, MRS BOSWICK *and her two* CHILDREN *are sitting by the meagre fire.*

She looks desperately anxious and is wringing her hands.

There's a key in the lock and MR BOSWICK *lets himself in.*

She kisses him and helps remove his hat and scarf.

BOSWICK*'s expression is strange – a kind of serious delight.*

MRS BOSWICK. Well? Is it good or bad?

BOSWICK. Bad.

MRS BOSWICK. We are quite ruined?

BOSWICK. No, there's hope yet, my love.

MRS BOSWICK. If he relents there is!

BOSWICK. He's past relenting!

He gnaws at his knuckle, on the verge of hysteria.

He's dead!

MRS BOSWICK *gasps, then laughs, then covers her mouth.*

MRS BOSWICK. Lord forgive me but I'm glad! Glad!

BOSWICK. What the half-drunken woman whom I told you of last night said to me, when I tried to see him and obtain yet another delay and what I thought was a mere excuse to avoid me, turns out to have been quite true. He was not only very ill, but dying, then.

MRS BOSWICK. Who gets our debt?

BOSWICK. I don't know. But before that time we shall be ready with the money; and even though we were not, it would be a bad fortune indeed to find so merciless a creditor in his successor. We may sleep tonight with light hearts, my love!

The scene darkens.

SCROOGE *looks wretched. He's seen emotion connected to the death, alright.* Pleasure.

SCROOGE. Let me see some tenderness connected with a death or that dark chamber, Spirit, which we left just now, will be for ever present to me.

The GHOST *turns. And there's a voice in the darkness. Quiet, tremulous…*

Scene Six

PETER (*voice-over*). 'And he took a child, and set him in the midst of them… and when he had taken him in his arms, he said unto them – Whosoever shall receive one of such children in my name, receiveth me…'

The lights go up – on the Cratchit home. PETER is reading aloud from a Bible.

MRS CRATCHIT is sewing some black material by the light of the fire. BELINDA, GRACE and EDWIN are sitting at her feet.

MRS CRATCHIT gives a little sob and puts down her work. Her hand flies to her eyes.

MRS CRATCHIT. The… the colour hurts my eyes.

SCROOGE looks at the corner of the fireplace. TINY TIM's crutch lies unclaimed in its accustomed place.

MRS CRATCHIT gathers herself.

They're all right now. It makes them weak by candlelight and I wouldn't show weak eyes to your father when he comes home, for the world. It must be near his time.

PETER. Past it rather. But I think he's walked a little slower than he used, these few last evenings.

They all stare into space.

MRS CRATCHIT (*faltering*). I have known him walk with… I have known him walk with Tiny Tim very fast indeed.

PETER. And me too. Often.

EDWIN. Me too.

MRS CRATCHIT. But he was no trouble – no trouble. Was he? Bless him – And there is your father at the door!

BOB comes in. He gives a weak smile and the children all embrace him. But there's a dreadful quiet about it all.

BOB. Hello, my dears. And how are you getting on?

GRACE *holds up some of the black material. They are funeral arm-bands.*

Oh, that's good work! You'll be finished long before Sunday.

MRS CRATCHIT. Sunday? You went today then, Robert?

BOB *sits down by the fire.*

BOB. Yes, my dear. I wish you could have gone. It would have done you good to see how green a place it is. But you'll see it often. I promised him that I would walk there on a Sunday and…

He looks away quickly.

You'll never guess who I saw today, my dear! Mr Scrooge's nephew! I can't have spoken to him more than half a dozen times but he greeted me like an old friend and seeing that I was… just a little down, you know asked what was the matter. On which – for he is the pleasantest-spoken gentleman you ever heard, I told him. 'I am heartily sorry for it, Mr Cratchit,' he said, 'and heartily sorry for your good wife.' By the by, how he ever knew that, I don't know.

MRS CRATCHIT. Knew what?

BOB. That you were a good wife.

PETER. Everybody knows that!

BOB. Very well observed, my boy. 'Heartily sorry,' he said, 'for your good wife. If I can be of service to you in any way,' he said, giving me his card, 'that's where I live. Pray come to me.' Now, it wasn't for the sake of anything he might be able to do for us, so much as for his kind way, that this was quite delightful. It really seemed as if he had known our Tiny Tim, and felt with us.

MRS CRATCHIT. I'm sure he's a good soul.

BOB. You would be surer of it, my dear, if you saw and spoke to him. I shouldn't be at all surprised mark what I say, if he got Peter a better situation.

PETER. Get along with you!

BOB. It's just as likely as not one of these days – though there's plenty of time for that, my dear. But however and whenever we part from one another, I am sure we shall none of us forget poor Tiny Tim, shall we, or this first parting that there was among us.

EDWIN. Never, Dad.

MRS CRATCHIT *holds him tight.*

BOB. I'm very happy. Very happy.

SCROOGE. Oh God... *God...*

BOB pats her on the back and pulls away, then, looking towards the stairs, gathers himself.

He mounts the stairs. SCROOGE *looks at the* GHOST *and they're suddenly upstairs in a tiny, dark bedroom.*

A single candle burns by the little bed. On it lies TINY TIM, *at peace.*

He looks down at the floor. BOB *comes in. With difficulty, he makes his way to the bedside and sits down. He looks at the little boy and bends to kiss his forehead.*

He sits back and smiles.

Then, all at once, BOB *breaks down into a terrible, ragged sobbing.*

BOB. My little, little child! My little child!

SCROOGE *turns away. Lights dim.*

SCROOGE. Spectre – something informs me that our parting moment is at hand. I know it, but I know not how. Tell me what man that was whom we saw lying dead!

They are suddenly on the move.

Scene Seven

SCROOGE *looks about. They're in a churchyard. Walled in by houses, overrun by grass and weeds, choked up with too much burying.*

Trembling, SCROOGE *advances into the dreadful place. He can hardly bear to look at the* GHOST *which has stopped before one particular grave and is pointing downwards.*

SCROOGE. Before... before I draw nearer to that stone to which you point, answer me one question. Are these the shadows of the things that will be, or are they shadows of things that *may* be, only?

Still, the GHOST *points down.*

Men's courses will foreshadow certain ends, to which, if persevered in, they must lead. But if the courses be departed from, the ends will change. Say it is thus with what you show me!

The GHOST *does not stir.*

SCROOGE *creeps forward to look at the name on the tomb.*

It is, of course, his own name: EBENEZER SCROOGE!

SCROOGE. I am that wretched man upon the bed! No, Spirit! Oh no, no, no!

The GHOST*'s finger does not move.* SCROOGE *hurls himself at its feet.*

(*Desperate.*) Good Spirit! Your nature intercedes for me, and pities me. Assure me that I yet may change these shadows you have shown me, by an altered life!

He clutches at the GHOST*'s hand and it tries to pull away.*

SCROOGE *persists and grabs desperately at the folds of the* GHOST*'s robes.*

The robes fall away revealing beneath – JACOB MARLEY*!*

SCROOGE *gasps.*

MARLEY. I tried to warn you, Ebenezer! Why did you not heed me? Why?

SCROOGE. But I will! I shall! Say it's not too late!

For answer MARLEY *merely looks up – as a HUGE chain begins to descend from above! It's three times the size of the one* MARLEY *bears himself. And it settles on* SCROOGE *like the suffocating tentacles of a monstrous creature.*

SCROOGE *scrabbles desperately at the chain as it swamps him.*

(*Sobbing.*) I will honour Christmas in my heart, and try to keep it all the year. I will live in the Past, the Present, and the Future. The Spirits of all three shall strive within me. I will not shut out the lessons that they teach. Oh, tell me I may sponge away the writing on this stone!

Blackout.

ACT FIVE

Scene One

SCROOGE *opens his eyes to find he is wrapped up in his own bed-curtains.*

He falls out of bed and looks around, gasping. Pale morning light – bright with snow – is filtering through the dirty panes of his window.

SCROOGE *claps his hands together as in prayer.*

SCROOGE. I'm alive! Oh God. I'm *alive*! Oh Jacob Marley! Heaven, and the Christmas Time be praised for this! I say it on my knees, old Jacob, on my *knees*.

He shoots a look at the bed-curtains.

They are not torn down! They are not torn down, rings and all. They are here – *I am here* – the shadows of the things that would have been, may be dispelled. They will be! I know they will!

He leaps up and staggers to the dresser where a chipped jug and bowl sit.

I don't know what to do! Haha! A good wash!

He lifts up the bowl and the water is frozen. He smiles, lifts out the ice and dashes it to the floor.

Haha! No time for bathing! Unless it's an ice bath! Clothes, clothes…

He drags his clothes from a table.

Oh awful! Horrid!

He throws them away.

Wonderfully awful! Wonderfully horrid! I don't know what to do!

I'm as light as a feather, I am as happy as an angel, I'm as merry as a schoolboy! I'm as giddy as a drunken man! A merry Christmas to everybody! A happy New Year to all the world!

He dashes into the parlour.

There's the saucepan that the gruel was in! There's the door, by which the Ghost of Jacob Marley entered. There's the corner where the Ghost of Christmas Present sat. There's the window where I saw the wandering Spirits. It's all right, it's all true, it all happened. Ha ha ha!

And he starts to laugh hysterically till his face is wet with tears.

I don't know what day of the month it is. I don't know how long I've been among the Spirits. I don't know anything. I'm quite a baby. Never mind. I don't care. I'd rather be a baby.

He laughs again, then stops in wonder as the church bells begin to peal madly.

Oh, what a blessed din!

He races to the window and throws it open. It's a bright, clear, freezing morning.

SCROOGE *breathes in the air as if it was wine. A* BOY *in his Sunday best is trudging through the snow outside.*

(*Calling.*) What's today?

BOY. Eh?

SCROOGE. What's today, my fine fellow?

BOY. Today? Why, Christmas Day!

SCROOGE. It's Christmas Day! I haven't missed it. The Spirits have done it all in one night. They can do anything they like. Of course they can. Of course they can.

Hello, my fine fellow!

BOY. Hello!

SCROOGE. Do you know the poulterer's, in the next street but one, at the corner?

BOY. I should hope I did!

SCROOGE. An intelligent boy! A remarkable boy! Do you know whether they've sold the prize turkey that was hanging up there – not the little prize turkey: the big one?

BOY. What, the one as big as me?

SCROOGE (*delighted*). What a delightful boy! It's a pleasure to talk to him. Yes, my buck.

BOY. It's hanging there now.

SCROOGE. Is it? Go and buy it.

BOY. Walk-*er*!

SCROOGE. No, no, I am in earnest. Go and buy it, and tell them to bring it here, that I may give them the direction where to take it. Come back with the man, and I'll give you a shilling. Come back with him in less than five minutes and I'll give you half-a-crown!

BOY. Half a – !

And he's off like a shot.

SCROOGE. I'll send it to Bob Cratchit's! He shan't know who sends it. It's twice the size of Tiny Tim! Now, where does he live? Camden Town, Camden Town...

He starts pulling open drawers and disinters dozens of mouldering papers. He throws them about, laughing his head off.

Scene Two

NARRATOR. Shaving was not an easy task, for his hand continued to shake very much – and shaving requires attention, even when you don't dance while you are at it. But if he had cut the end of his nose off, he would have put a piece of sticking-plaster over it, and been quite satisfied. He dressed himself 'all in his best,' and at last got out into the streets.

SCROOGE *opens the front door, now with his old coat over his night-shirt and carrying a label.*

The BOY *is approaching with* TOM *the poulterer who's got a huge turkey in his arms.*

SCROOGE *beams at them, then notices the lion's head knocker on the door and pats it fondly.*

I shall love it as long as I live! Scarcely ever looked at it before. What an honest expression it has in its face. It's a wonderful knocker. Here's the turkey. Hello! Whoop! How are you?

TOM. Mr Scrooge?

SCROOGE. Yes, yes!

(*With relish.*) Merry Christmas!

TOM. The lad said it was you but I hardly believed –

SCROOGE *hands the label and a purse of money to* TOM.

'Ere, this is far too much, sir!

SCROOGE. Keep it! Keep it! Take a cab to Camden Town or the weight of that bird'll see you off!

TOM. Thank you, sir! A merry Christmas, sir!

He makes to go back inside. The BOY *looks downcast.* SCROOGE *notices.*

SCROOGE. Heavens! A little matter of half a – (*Clears his throat.*) Half a sovereign, wasn't it?

The BOY *gawps.*

NARRATOR. The people were by this time pouring forth, as he had seen them with the Ghost of Christmas Present, and walking with his hands behind him, Scrooge regarded every one with a delighted smile. He looked so irresistibly pleasant, in a word, that three or four good-humoured fellows said, 'Good morning, sir! A merry Christmas to you!' And Scrooge said often afterwards, that of all the blithe sounds he had ever heard, those were the blithest in his ears.

SCROOGE *suddenly spots* MRS BOONE, *who tried to persuade him into charity only the night before.*

SCROOGE *looks ashamed, then brightens.*

SCROOGE. My dear lady! How do you do. I hope you succeeded in your endeavours yesterday. It was so very kind of you. A merry Christmas to you, madam!

He grabs MRS BOONE *by both hands. She looks nonplussed.*

MRS BOONE. Mr Scrooge?

SCROOGE. Yes, that's my name, and I fear it may not be pleasant to you. Allow me to ask your pardon. And will you have the goodness to accept –

He whispers in MRS BOONE*'s ear.*

MRS BOONE. Good God! Mr Scrooge, are you serious?

SCROOGE. If you please. Not a farthing less. A great many back-payments are included in it, I assure you. Will you do me that favour?

MRS BOONE. I will!

SCROOGE *doffs his hat and then stops dead. Across the way from him he sees:* BELLE.

For a long moment they stare at one another. His heart leaps – is there still a chance?

Then her husband, the FATHER *we saw before, emerges from the crowd and gently takes her arm. He doesn't notice* SCROOGE.

BELLE *smiles sadly towards* SCROOGE *and he gives her a tiny wave of the hand.*

Then he melts away into the crowd.

Over this: a church congregation belting out 'O Come All Ye Faithful'.

Scene Three

The wintry afternoon is creeping in and SCROOGE *is pacing up and down outside his nephew's house.*

There's the sound of laughter and music from within but SCROOGE *is nervous.*

He suddenly makes a dash for the door and knocks half a dozen times before he can change his mind.

The door is opened by a PARLOUR MAID.

SCROOGE. Is… is your master at home, my dear?

PARLOUR MAID. Yes, sir.

SCROOGE. Where is he, my love?

PARLOUR MAID. He's in the dining-room, sir, along with the mistress. I'll show you upstairs, if you please.

SCROOGE. Thank you. He knows me. I'll just go in, my dear.

Everyone is as before, about to play games. SCROOGE *pops his head round the door. They're playing Blind Man's Buff.*

FRED. Who's that?

FRED *gropes his way to the door and finds…* SCROOGE!

SCROOGE. It's I. Your Uncle Scrooge. Will you let me in, Fred?

FRED. Well, bless my soul! Let you in!

He shakes SCROOGE *vigorously by the hand.*

My dear uncle, I hardly knew you! You look –

SCROOGE. Happy? I am. Oh I am. As happy as only an old sinner could be on this wonderful day!

CAROLINE *is staring at him.*

And who is this? As if I couldn't guess. Why, my dear, how lovely you are. I am so very pleased to meet you.

CAROLINE. Fred has spoken of you so often. I never thought –

SCROOGE. No more did I. I'm not much of a Christmas present, I'm afraid but if I may – belatedly – accept your invitation to dinner…?

CAROLINE. Of course!

FRED *is smiling fit to burst.*

Oh, of course!

She embraces SCROOGE *as we fade on them, glowing in the gorgeous candle-light…*

Scene Four

NARRATOR. Oh but he was early at the office next morning! He was early there. If he could only be there first, and catch Bob Cratchit coming late! That was the thing he had set his heart upon…

BONNIFACE *the cab-man sits on the snow-covered steps of* SCROOGE'*s office. He looks absolutely wretched and has clearly had a miserable Christmas.*

Suddenly, SCROOGE *comes pelting round the corner, pursued by a crowd of* BOYS.

BONNIFACE *gawps as* SCROOGE *bends to make a snowball and hurls it back at the* BOYS.

Laughing, SCROOGE *ducks a snowball and trots towards his office door.*

He doesn't notice BONNIFACE *until he almost has the key in the lock.*

SCROOGE. Oh!

BONNIFACE. Mr Scrooge...

SCROOGE. Oh, it's you! The cab-man.

BONNIFACE. Yes, sir. I have not slept, sir.

(*A last appeal*.) For the sake of Christmas –

SCROOGE. Christmas was yesterday, Mr Bonniface. And a little matter of...

He takes out his pocket book.

Seven pounds, three shillings and six has fallen due! So...

He reaches into his purse and begins to count out some notes.

...five six, seven pounds. Oh, and here's another twenty pounds to see you right.

Are we all square?

BONNIFACE. Eh?

SCROOGE. A merry Christmas, my lad.

He holds up his pocket book and rips it into little pieces.

BONNIFACE *looks at the money and grins.*

BONNIFACE (*sincerely*). God bless you, Mr Scrooge. God *bless* you!

He wrings SCROOGE's *hand and darts off.*

SCROOGE *is delighted. He lets himself into the office.*

Scene Five

The office. BOB CRATCHIT*'s chair is unoccupied.* SCROOGE *looks at the big clock which is just striking nine.*

SCROOGE. Oh, but Bob Cratchit's late! Dear me. What shall I do?

He laughs to himself and tries to assume his old frown.

(*Rehearsing.*) 'Cratchit! What time do you call this?'

(*Tries again.*) 'Cratchit! What is this meaning of – '

(*Laughs.*) Don't think I can do it any more. Been smiling so much. Now then...

He shuffles into his counting office and takes up his pen.

BOB *comes flying inside, panting, taking off his hat and scarf and begins writing all in one movement, hoping that* SCROOGE *hasn't noticed.*

Cratchit! What do you mean by coming here at this time of day?

Wearily, BOB *gets up and presents himself in the doorway of* SCROOGE*'s office.*

BOB. I'm very sorry, sir. I am behind my time.

SCROOGE. You are? Yes, I think you are. Full eighteen and a half minutes. Step this way, if you please.

BOB *shuffles in, like a man on his way to the gallows.*

BOB. It's only once a year, sir. It shall not be repeated. I was making rather merry yesterday, sir.

SCROOGE (*low and dangerous*). Now, I'll tell you what, my friend. I am not going to stand this sort of thing any longer. And therefore –

He leaps to his feet and embraces BOB.

– and therefore I am about to raise your salary!

BOB *stumbles backwards and gropes for the big steel ruler.*

It's all right! It's all right! There's no need to fetch the straight-waistcoat and the men from the Bedlam! A merry Christmas, Bob!

He slaps BOB *on the back.*

A merrier Christmas, Bob, my dear fellow, than I have ever given you!

I'll raise your salary, and endeavour to assist your struggling family, and we will discuss your affairs this very afternoon, over a Christmas bowl of smoking bishop, Bob. Make up the fires, and buy another coal-scuttle before you dot another 'I', Bob Cratchit!

He bursts out laughing and then, after a moment, BOB *does too.*

The stage darkens and we hear the voice of the NARRATOR...

NARRATOR (*voice-over*). Scrooge was better than his word. He did it all, and infinitely more...

Scene Six

Lights fade up on the NARRATOR. *We now see that he has been telling the story to an enraptured group of* CHILDREN *who sit around his feet in a cosy Edwardian parlour.*

NARRATOR. And to Tiny Tim – *who did not die –*

– he was a second father. He became as good a friend, as good a master, and as good a man, as the good old city knew, or any other good old city, town, or borough, in the good old world. Some people laughed to see the alteration in him, but he let them laugh. His own heart laughed: and that was quite enough for him.

He had no further dealings with Spirits, but lived upon the
Total Abstinence Principle, ever afterwards; and it was
always said of him that he knew how to keep Christmas well,
if any man alive possessed the knowledge.

His eyes brim with tears and he glances towards the fire.

ELDERLY WOMAN. My dear!

An ELDERLY WOMAN *has popped her head round the
door. He doesn't seem to hear her.*

Timothy?

It's time.

The NARRATOR *looks up and smiles warmly.*

And the CHILDREN *whoop delightedly, jumping to their
feet and rushing through into the dining room.*

The NARRATOR *gets to his feet with the aid of a stick and
takes his wife's arm.*

*Double doors open onto a magical Christmas spread, the
table covered in gorgeous trimmings and mouth-watering
food.*

And, in the centre is a magnificent cooked goose.

The CHILDREN *scramble to their places, their assembled
elders are already seated.*

The NARRATOR *claps his hands in joy.*

NARRATOR. Oh! There never *was* such a goose!

Smiling, he sits down and raises a glass of wine.

A merry Christmas, my dears.

ALL. Merry Christmas!

NARRATOR. God bless us. *Every one.*

End.

www.nickhernbooks.co.uk

facebook.com/nickhernbooks

twitter.com/nickhernbooks